CHASING JAMES GANDOLFINI

CHASING JAMES GANDOLFINI

A Memoir

Donna Bluze

Full Court Press
Englewood Cliffs, New Jersey

First Edition

Copyright © 2020 by Donna Bluze

All rights reserved. No part of this book may be reproduced or transmitted in any form or by any means electronic or mechanical, including by photocopying, by recording, or by any information storage and retrieval system, without the express permission of the author, except where permitted by law.

Published in the United States of America
by Full Court Press, 601 Palisade Avenue,
Englewood Cliffs, NJ 07632
fullcourtpress.com

Print ISBN 978-1-946989-64-2
Ebook ISBN 978-1-946989-68-0
Library of Congress Control Number: 2020908239

Editing and book design by Barry Sheinkopf

Cover art, by the author, photographed on the last day of shooting for *The Sopranos*. The author gratefully acknowledges Holsten's Ice Cream Parlor for permission to reproduce.

Dedication

Above all, I would like to thank God and his son Jesus Christ. I prayed for you to help me, and you did. I will be forever grateful.

To Dawn and Angelique—you are two incredible human beings, kind and giving to everyone in your path. Thanks for your support, encouragement, and true friendship.

And to Karen, thank you for your words of wisdom, caring above and beyond, and being in the room when my little girl was born. I'll be forever grateful.

"And if a house be divided against itself, that house cannot stand" *(Mark 3:25)*
"United, we stand; divided, we fall."

TABLE OF CONTENTS

Missed Opportunity, *9*
Billy, *13*
Big Dog, *24*
Ninety-Nine Percent, *28*
Dana, *32*
Uncle Leo, *35*
Karen, *37*
Take Two, *40*
Where Were You?, *46*
Will Smith, *49*
Rise and Shine, *56*
Law and Order SVU, *59*
Selective Hearing, *64*
Robin Williams, *68*
Cloud Nine, *76*
Black Hole, *82*
Euphoria, *91*
Five Little Words, *95*
Bonnie and Clyde, *99*
Paranoia, *103*
John Travolta and Radio Man, *109*
The Call, *114*
Crutch, *118*
Green, *121*
Flam, *124*
Lucky, *127*

It's Calling My Name, *130*
Down for the Count, *134*
The Test Dream, *137*
Viral Spiral, *140*
The Sopranos, *142*
Divine Intervention, *149*
Rock Bottom, *153*
Holsten's, *155*
Out of the Fog, *159*
Satin Dolls, *161*
Nurse Ratchet, *165*
Goodbye, *170*
L'ultimo Capitolo, *173*

Acknowledgments, 177

The Little Boy With The Bright Red Hair

Why are you following me every day?
Don't you have somewhere else to play?
Okay, but. . .we must crochet.
Yes, he smiled and came my way.
House, I said, next we'll play.
I'll get my dolls. Right here—please stay.
Where are the boys? It's snowing outside.
Let's get the sled. I'll give you a ride.
Mom and Dad are taking us all to the hill.
All six together, it should be a thrill.
Sit on my lap—I'll hold you real tight.
We'll laugh and cling on, with all our might
And slide down the hill with incredible speed. . .
Having him with me was fun, don't you know?
His bright red hair, all covered with snow.
Today was different when I thought of you.
You must accept it. What else can you do?
I want to pound the floor and make it crack.
If I pound and pound, maybe you'll come back.
Many years have passed, there is no choice.
Even now I can still hear. . .your sweet voice.
My heart still aches, and I don't often share
about my little brother. . .with the bright red hair.

MY VISION

I have had a vision for this book for some time now. I was inspired by two people, Jim Carey and Albert Einstein. Jim Carey, a successful actor/comedian, wrote a ten-million-dollar check to himself before he was famous. He post-dated it for ten years and kept it in his wallet. While he was struggling to make it, he parked his car up on the Hollywood Hills overlooking Los Angeles and pictured his dreams coming true...and they did.

Albert Einstein said, "Don't fall in love with a person, fall in love with an idea." I had given my heart away a few times only to be let down, so I took his advice. I put my love into the idea of publishing a children's book that I wrote many years ago. I thought it had an important message to send into the world, so I found a way to make it happen. I didn't want to stop there; I needed to tell another story.

Chasing James Gandolfini is based on a true story—*my story*. I already have the movie planned, the actors I would like in it, and the potential directors. If done right, this movie would be something that I, and everyone else, would love to see. It's original and sheds light on one of the most talented actors of our time. I have all the music picked out too, but only one thing that is a must: While the credits are rolling at the end, "Africa," by the band Toto, must be playing. That's how I have always envisioned it. I guess this book is my post-dated check—just me and my story, waiting for my dream to come true.

INTRODUCTION

Driving home from East Hanover, New Jersey, after a long day at work, I patiently wait until I can see the Empire State Building lit up in the distance. I wonder what color it will be tonight. That's a sight that gives me a warm feeling that home is near—home, a small town in New Jersey that has given me some of the best and worst memories of my life.

One night, I was just staring at the road ahead when I began to drift off into a slight haze. It was like right at that moment, for the first time, I was mentally aware where I truly was in my life, and I couldn't believe how many years had passed. I felt for the first time conscious of it.

I started to think all I had been through and somehow managed to overcome: abuse and severe mental bullying from grade school until high school, the depths of depression, the untimely death of my youngest brother, and a bout with drug addiction. I don't want to leave out the year and a half of obesity due to medication, either. It's amazing how differently you're treated when you are overweight. It was very sad—not for me, but to see how cruel people can be to others.

I've lived all these lives, worn all these hats, filled all these shoes. If Einstein was right when he said, "The only source of knowledge is experience," I can say that I was very well educated in all those situations, because I have lived them. Did I learn from my mistakes? Yes. Will you? Maybe, maybe not.

We have all had heartache in our lives, and skeletons in our closets. Even Tony Soprano had problems, so much so he felt he needed therapy. In came Doctor Melfi, a female psychiatrist he sought for help. A move like that could be very dangerous for a mob boss, but for him it was worth the risk.

He suffered from panic attacks that led to him passing out. A lot of this stemmed from his childhood and unresolved issues he had with his mother.

It didn't surprise me that I was drawn to this character— a strong man, bad boy if you will, a protector, that no one would ever dare cross, putting on a strong front while struggling underneath. A good father who loves his kids, wrestling with depression and a past that has caught up with him. The scenario sounds all too familiar; I guess the trick is, how are we all going to handle it?

Tony landed in a doctor's office for stress. As a child, I got there because I would constantly tell my mother, "I feel like I'm not here." I can picture it now—my mother, me, and the doctor in the room. The doctor asked, "Okay, young lady, what seems to be the problem?"

My mother looked him straight in the eye and said, "She feels like she's not here."

I now realize I must have been lightheaded from all the stress I endured trying to get an education.

One of my favorite episodes of The Sopranos was the one around Christmas. Tony had a list of things he needed to do for the holidays. Prior to that, his sister Janice, played by the remarkable actress Aida Turturro, stole a prosthetic leg from a Russian woman who used to take care of their mother. Her Russian relatives beat her up. One of the things Tony added to his run-of-the-mill Christmas list besides "gift for Carm" and "transfer cannolis" was "Janice's Russian." It was right there among all the other holiday chores. Crossing them off throughout his day, we wondered, would Tony get to it? Getting involved with the Russians is something he did not want to do. It wasn't until Janice was watching the news with tears in her eyes that, in my opinion, she felt truly loved by her brother.

In another great episode, I'm sure I wasn't the only one whispering under my breath, "Tell him! Tell him!" when Tony asked Dr. Melfi what was wrong after she was raped. You know she wanted to. We wanted her to. They say inner anger is depression, and outer anger is rage. I guess seeing a therapist might be a wise choice for a lot of people. I've seen a few, but only one like Dr. Melfi.

One school memory sticks out in my head to this day. I was about nine and walking down the hall of my grammar school. I was always nervous, anticipating an unpleasant encounter with someone. Slam! I felt it right between the shoulder blades, so hard that my neck jerked back and my body went surging forward. I just about kept my balance.

Still in shock, the kids passed me, laughing. It was not an unusual occurrence, nor were other types of physical and mental bullying that filled my days. Where were the teachers and our principal? Didn't they know the impact such abuse would have on our lives? Why didn't they protect us?

And where were my balls? Why didn't I knock the shit out of them? These are the questions I often asked myself.

I've always wished I could go back, knowing what I know now, and rescue my self-esteem and, more importantly, my self-worth.

There were a lot of casualties in my school district. Some had it much worse. But it was a long time ago I'm told—get over it.

Get over it? *I must take three different antidepressants a day and still fight my depression. Weight gain is a struggle because of the meds; I long ago said goodbye to the nice body I once had.*

So I still live with the aftereffects of my childhood. I can hear Tony Soprano's mother Livia now utter her memorable phrase, "Oh, poor you," played so brilliantly by the late actress Nancy Marchand.

I guess dwelling on the past is not the answer. We've all been dealt a hand of cards in life. Einstein also said, "Life is like riding a bicycle. To keep your balance, you must keep moving." So that's what I do. That's what we all have to do.

1
MISSED OPPORTUNITY

I WORKED AT A HAIR SHOP in Lodi, New Jersey, for a good twenty years—at first, full time, but then just on the weekends to make a little extra money. We all loved watching *The Sopranos*. After all, the infamous Bada Bing strip club, aka Satin Dolls, was practically around the corner. Filming was done all over our area. We always talked about how perfect our little mini-mall would be to film, especially considering in the '80s it was once a big hangout for...I guess Tony Soprano would call it the "waste management" crew. They were all nice guys. Everyone knew them, and everyone loved them.

My friend from the shop told me, "If they ever offer you anything, don't say no. It would be an insult."

I was in my twenties. What did I know? There was always a man in the back of the deli in a crisp, well-cut black suit and a black hat. His hair was white as snow. I assumed he was very important in the waste management industry. One day, he saw me in the deli and motioned me over.

Surprisingly, I wasn't afraid, so I went.

"What're you doing this weekend?" he asked in a raspy voice.

"My brother's getting married, and I'm going to his wedding."

He took out his wallet, slid out a crisp hundred-dollar bill, and handed it to me.

"Go get yourself something nice," he said with a half-smile.

"Thank you!" I said, without having time to think about it, I smiled at him, and went back to work.

What else could I do? When it began to sink in what had just happened, the first thing I thought was "blood money," but then I realized I was a little melodramatic. He was just being nice, and I didn't want to insult him. I do have to admit—at that time, on that day, it was nice getting a hundred bucks.

Years later, I was still working at the shop but only part-time. I had to take some time off (for the first time) because, while I was pregnant with my daughter, I was suffering horrible prepartum depression. It was impossible for me to function at any level, let alone cut hair.

After giving birth, I slowly tried to pull myself out of it. Feeling a little better, I thought I would venture out and stop by the salon. I wanted to see everyone and was in desperate need of a trim. As I sat waiting for my appointment, my gaze drifted around the shop. I passed one of the girls' stations but then had to go back and do a quick double take.

"What's *that*?" I asked. "Is that a picture of James Gandolfini with Genie in front of the shop? How did she get this?"

One of the new shampoo girls told me that they'd filmed a scene from the Sopranos there about a month before.

"*What?* When? Are you kidding me? Why didn't anyone call me?"

Still suffering the after-effects of what I had been through, I really felt bad. My eyes began to tear up. I'd worked with these people for years. They knew how much I loved *The Sopranos*. I couldn't believe not one of them had thought to call me. It would have been so exciting to see James Gandolfini and the taping of the show. Just to be there would have been amazing for me. I had no words to describe how disappointed I was.

It was the episode when Tony is on a payphone, telling Adriana that Christopher was in the hospital because of an apparent suicide attempt. Actually, she was being set up to be killed. From what I was told, they had to install a fake payphone in our parking lot. You can see all the stores in the background, including our shop.

"Sorry, Don, we didn't think of it. They wouldn't let anyone near the filming anyway," one of my ex co-workers said.

Really? I thought. It looks like *someone* managed. They don't know how I am. I am like Chevy Chase in *Fletch*. I can take on any persona, get in anywhere—nobody questions me. When my manager wants something done, she sends me. When she comes across a person that has some emotional issue and it needs to be handled, I'm her girl. I *know* people. . .I would at least have gotten a picture with my favorite actor.

A month later, I returned to the shop to get my hair colored. I looked around and noticed a lot of new faces. I hadn't heard, but the shop had been sold and changed hands. At the desk, I saw a pretty woman named Veronica. She had blonde hair and was very friendly.

"Veronica," I asked, "has *The Sopranos* been filming anywhere around here lately? They did film in this mall a couple of months ago, but my co-workers didn't think to call me. I was out having my baby. I was so upset."

"No, not that I know of, but my brother John owns a talent agency and they cast extras for *The Sopranos*."

"Really? He *does?*" I exclaimed, with an eager, surprised look on my face.

"Here's the number," she said, handing me a piece of paper. "Why don't you give him a call today? His name is John."

"He does *really?* Are you kidding me?"

"Really, he does—also for a lot of other TV and movie projects."

After my hair was done, I went to my car. Is this for real? I thought. I don't care, I'm calling. Unfolding the little slip of paper, I dialed the number.

"Good afternoon, Global Talent."

"Hello. Is John there?"

"This is him. How can I help you?"

2

BILLY

I WAS SEVENTEEN WHEN I TOOK Work Study in high school, a program that allowed me to take the required courses in the morning, leave, and go to work for the rest of the day. It was perfect for me. I could spend the least amount of time in school, counting the days I could leave for good.

It's ironic that, even though I left years ago, I have a dream to this day that I am waiting to graduate. I wonder in the dream, why didn't they plan the prom yet? I'm too old to be in school. We should be graduating. It's July—I should have graduated. *What is going* on? I can't tell you how many times I have had that same dream over the years.

Billy was a nineteen-year-old kid who worked for my friend's father as a plumber. He was a cross between John Travolta and James Dean, absolutely gorgeous. All the girls in town loved him. He had his own apartment, but from what his working buddy told me, a perfect date to him would be a six-pack and a motel room. I'd never been out on a date or had a boyfriend or any kind of sexual experience. I froze whenever I was near anybody I liked. I couldn't even talk. I didn't have any kind of confidence or self-esteem. It was forever lost in the classroom, lunchroom, playgrounds, and halls of my grade school. A girl going through her young years with no self-worth is a recipe for disaster.

I heard through the grapevine that Billy was thinking about asking me out. I think the head plumber, Bobby, thought it would be a good idea. Billy'd heard I was a little shy, so I had the feeling it wasn't on his list of priorities. He loved to go out on the weekends with his best friend Joey, hitting the clubs and looking for girls. I patiently waited, hoping he'd get around to it.

A couple of weeks later, I saw him talking to someone out a window from my girlfriend Gina's apartment building. He worked out of the basement, so it was a perfect way to bump into him casually. I looked up and said, "Hi Billy."

He said, "Hi, how are you?" I had turned away and continued walking, not knowing what else to say, when I heard him add, "Would you like to go see a movie sometime?"

I turned back around, smiled, said, "Okay," and continued walking.

I immediately ran upstairs to tell Gina. The first thing she asked me is what I was going to wear. She even tried to put together potential outfits from her closet. Gina was good at putting clothes together. She changed outfits three times a day. She was a one-woman fashion show.

Purple Rain was the movie of choice. He picked me up at my parents' house. My body was frozen with fear. He was so nice. He bought us some popcorn and drinks, and we slowly made our way down to our seats. I couldn't pay much attention to the movie because, while eating, I thought the crunching sound I was making was so loud everyone could hear. Billy, on the other hand, stared at the screen, the look on his face filled with emotion.

Driving in his car after leaving the theater, he went on about how he loved the movie. He said it reminded him a lot of his own life growing up. I was half listening to him, because I could see we were heading back to my parents' house. I knew what was coming next. I was so nervous. I never had kissed anyone before. I felt my legs actually shaking. He opened the door for me and let me out of the car, took my hand, and leaned my back against the side of the door. He put one hand around the small of my waist and the other around the back of my neck. I could feel my body trembling with fear. He leaned in and put his big full lips on mine. I closed my eyes. It was better than I imagined. So warm. . .so nice. . .I was in a dream. I started to drift off for a second. Then I felt something go in my mouth. *What? Why is he doing this? Is he sick?* I was confused. Why was he putting his tongue in my *mouth?* He was going in and out, back and forth. I couldn't keep up. Of course, now I know why and enjoy it immensely, but back then, naïve as I was, what a shocker.

The next morning, I woke up on cloud nine. I couldn't stop thinking about him. I was in love, or thought I was. Before he left, he had told me to call him the next day. I told myself, I'm such a dating expert now, I don't want to look so anxious, so I waited an extra day. When I did call, and he realized it was me, he sounded a little nervous. We didn't have caller ID then, so there was no way of knowing who was on the other line when you picked up the phone.

"Oh, hi," he said in a low whisper. "Listen...can I call you later?"

I said, "Okay," and he quickly hung up. I found out years later he was in bed with another girl.

My mother knew how happy I was but was afraid for me. She was worried that since I'd been rejected by my peers growing up, the first heartbreak might run a lot deeper than most. She knew I would be devastated if I did anything with Billy and it didn't work out, especially considering it would be my first time. She didn't think he was the kind of guy looking to settle down with just one girl. Looking back at pictures, I was very attractive but didn't know it think it or feel it back then. It's amazing how the way you feel about yourself can cloud your perception.

Billy and I went out again the following week. We had a great time. I didn't talk much but loved being with him. That time we ended up at his apartment. As we sat on his bed, my mother's words kept ringing in my ears: "Don't do anything you're going to regret."

He started kissing me, moving his tongue slowly in and out of mouth. His hands slowly started to rub my back, making their way slowly up my shirt. I put my hands on his and led them back down. He hugged me, kissed me on the cheek, and said, "Come on, it's late. We better get you home."

Home already? I thought.

Billy never called me after that night. I was not a happy camper. From what I heard, I was too quiet for him. His boss was also a friend of my father's, so I think he didn't want to get into a sticky situation. I still had hope, though, determined to be more of the kind of girl he liked. Luckily, he worked in the basement of Gina's apartment building, so I had a chance to see him again. I spent most of my time over there, hoping he would pass by with his truck. Sporting the stretch pants he loved, I would park in the farthest spot, so my chances would increase. When he saw me, he would beep and wave giving me that warm wide smile of his.

My heart was broken. I felt, at the time, why would he want me? I wasn't good enough for him. He'd gotten to know me and of course found out what everyone else had. How could I ever think that he would want *me* for his girlfriend? I know, it's pitiful, but that's what I thought at the time. It took years to make me feel that way, and twice as many to overcome.

One afternoon a couple of weeks later, I was sitting with Gina, having coffee at her kitchen table. She was by then seeing Billy's brother Noah. The doorbell rang. It wasn't unusual at Gina's—she had a lot of friends, told them to "stop by," and they always did. She went down to answer the door, and, to my surprise, Billy strolled in behind her as she made her way back into the kitchen.

"So what are you girls up to today?"

I froze. Gina did all the talking. I sat there like a zombie.

He looked at me after a while and said, "Don, can you

light my cigarette for me?"

Years ago, to light their cigarettes, smokers would sometimes put one in their mouth, turn on the stove, and lean over the burner to light it. I had seen people do it a couple of times. I smiled and took the cigarette from him. I put it in my mouth, turned on the flame, and leaned over the stove.

The next thing I knew, I heard a loud crackling noise. I'd set my hair on *fire!* My bangs were singed by the flame and fell to the floor in little pieces.

Billy shouted, "Are you fuckin' *retarded?* Are you *alright?* What's the *matter* with you?" I could see the look of terror in his eyes.

He was clearly upset. The abundance of hairspray I had on didn't help, but it *was* the '80s. Gina, on the other hand, proceeded to go into one of her panic-stricken laughing fits. It was the way her body would react to unexpected tragedies, even if they happened to her. I guess it was a coping mechanism.

All I kept hearing was, "Are you alright? Are you alright?"

My memory is a blank after that. To this day, I don't remember what happened next. I think I blocked it out. Can you blame me? I laugh at it now, but back then it was the most humiliating experience of my young life.

A COUPLE OF MONTHS WENT BY. Billy and Noah had since moved into one of the apartments downstairs. Gina had a young child, so we didn't get too many opportunities to go out. We made our own little party and spied out the front window to see when the boys would be back from their night of partying.

"Here they come!" Gina cried.

Quickly, we turned the music up and made sure we had a beer in our hands. We would start joking as if we were having the best time, which we usually were. Then a knock came at the door—always Noah.

"Hi, guys—you mind if I hang out with you?"

Of *course,* we don't mind, I thought. We've been waiting for you guys for the last six hours. Then the phone rang. I knew who it was. . .Billy.

"Hold on," I heard Gina say. Billy then asked me to come down to his apartment, and each time we would just kiss. He tried for more, but I stopped him. I just loved being with him and kissing. I didn't realize how frustrating that was for a nineteen-year-old man.

I was ready to leave when Noah said to me, "Don, I wouldn't run down there like a bunny every time he calls you."

I didn't listen. Back then, I thought, He must really miss me. He went out and didn't find anyone he liked better, so he had to rush back and be with me.

Billy was really patient with the whole just-kissing deal, but I think it was wearing thin. I thought the night went well. I was having such a great time. I asked him if he could slow-dance with me, so we did as he slowly kissed me.

He tried again for more. This time I said, "But you don't love me."

He said, "I *do* love you."

I knew he didn't. He hadn't called me in months other

than late at night and I didn't trust that he would after. I was afraid he would get what he wanted, and I would never see him again. I declined of course and we both fell asleep with me lying on his chest his arm wrapped tightly around me, just where I wanted to be.

THE NEXT MORNING, WE WOKE UP. I looked at him and said, "Good morning."

He did not look happy. I think when you are a nineteen-year-old boy and your hormones are raging, a smiling virgin is the last thing you want to see.

He said, "I think you should leave. I really don't want to see you anymore."

"Why? What did I do?" I felt my eyes tearing up.

"Just leave now, please," he said in a stern voice.

I was so upset. I got my things and headed for the door. I bumped into Noah outside. He was just leaving from Gina's. I had gotten him phone-line type key chains he wanted in the colors of the Italian flag. I said hi to him and told him I had the chains. As I handed them to him, I started to cry hysterically.

"Don. . .what's the matter? Why are you crying?"

He was so caring. Trying to talk through my blubbering breaths, I said, "Billy told me to leave the apartment and that he never wants to see me again."

"Why? What happened?"

"I wouldn't sleep with him." I was still crying.

At that moment, his understanding face turned angry—very, very, angry. He said, "I'll kill him."

Three hours later, I was up at Gina's, licking my

wounds, when the doorbell rang. It was Noah and Billy with Dunkin' Donuts.

As we all sat around the dining room table, you could cut the tension with a knife. You knew Billy *did not* want to be there. He sat straight ahead with a pouty look on his face while Noah and Gina did all the talking. At one point I heard him whisper to Noah, "See? She doesn't talk."

He was right, I didn't—so painfully shy and insecure, especially around him.

I took it hard. I cried to my mother. Of course, she had seen it coming, but she knew it could have been much worse. The way I felt about myself was all tied up in this guy. If he wanted to be with me, I felt good about myself; if he didn't, I felt like nothing.

Many weeks went by. I was really down because I hadn't seen or heard from Billy. Gina wanted to go out to dinner with Noah one Saturday night, so she asked if I could babysit, and I of course agreed. I was hoping that I might bump into him over there one day, hopefully not with another girl.

After the baby was in her crib sleeping, I lay down on the couch and began to watch television. I had started to drift off into a sleep when the phone rang. It was Billy! He knew I was babysitting and asked me if I wanted some company. I said, "Okay." I quickly checked my hair in the bathroom and started digging in my pocketbook for a breath mint.

A long time had passed since the donut incident. I missed him terribly. I couldn't wait to see him. I opened the door, and there he was, looking even better that I remembered. We said our hellos and sat down on the couch next to each other.

I tried to be more talkative. I had even written down a list of potential subjects to talk to him about just in case I saw him again, but there had been no time to review.

It turned out I didn't need the list. I was a lot more relaxed that night. We talked, joked around, and watched TV while we snuggled under a warm blanket. You know I was loving it.

Then, out of the corner of my eye, I saw him staring at me. I turned and looked at him. Our eyes met and he leaned in and kissed me, gently and slowly. He told me that he missed me and asked me if I missed him.

"Yes," I replied as he slowly started to kiss my neck. This went on for a long time. He was being so sweet and tender. We had still been under the covers when he started, and then he was slowly moving his hands up and down the sides of my body. He kissed my mouth, while circling both my nipples through my blouse with his index fingers, and lightly pinching them.

He started to slip his tongue in and out of my mouth. I loved his tongue now. I loved him. He kept my shirt on but continued pinching my nipples through my shirt, this time pulling gently on them. He pulled down my pants slowly, kissing my stomach, leaving my underwear on. He kept kissing me, my neck, my lips, my mouth. . . .

Then he dipped his head under the covers. He eased down my underwear, kissing me slowly below my belly button down to my inner thigh, and gently spread my legs. I was soaking wet. I couldn't believe what he was doing—

my body felt so much pleasure, I couldn't stay still, I could barely stand it, but I didn't want him to stop. What are you *doing* to me? I wondered. I felt a surging heat rise throughout my whole body. My neck and back arched in a stiffened position, and my whole body began to tremble uncontrollably. I couldn't believe it. As strange as it sounds, at that age, I was not aware of how a man can pleasure a woman. All I knew was that it felt amazing.

He looked at me after then whispered in my ear, "That was all for you."

That's all we did that night. We fell asleep holding each other, with me on his chest with his arm around me like always—just where I wanted to be.

I WAS IN LOVE WITH BILLY for many years but luckily listened to the voice of my mother. He went on to be with a lot more girls. Some of them I even knew through Gina. I was hurt, but not as much as I would have been if I had lost my virginity that night.

I went on to meet a musician at the age of twenty-one. He had once been the same type of guy as Billy, but he was six years older than me. It was perfect, because he had grown out of his "player ways" and turned out to be a good first boyfriend. Billy became a very successful businessman. He built his own plumbing company from the ground up. He married a girl a bit younger and had some kids.

I did not know at that time that our paths would cross again in the future. . .and that the course of my life would change forever.

3

BIG DOG

I HAVE THREE BROTHERS. One is in heaven, the other is a year older than me, and then there's the eldest, Bill, aka "Big Dog." I don't know who gave him the nickname; maybe he gave it to himself, but it stuck. Bill lives life according to a master plan. He's a great brother, but if he doesn't approve of how your living your life or whom you're seeing, he wouldn't be shy or inadvertent in letting you know. If he thinks you're wasting your time in a relationship that is not good for you and going nowhere, he might approach you with a sly smile and a deck of old maid cards, and ask you if you want to play. He would actually have the cards.

"Very funny, Bill."

"Listen to Big Dog if you want your life to go right," he has said on more than one occasion. "Big Dog is always right."

Old Maid—yes, it's a joke, but sometimes when a member of your family says something that hits home, even in kidding, it hurts twice as much. I think that is why, even though Tony Soprano was basically a murderer, bad guy if you will, we fell in love with him because on more than one occasion, his character showed his vulnerable side.

"He never had the makings of a varsity athlete." In one of my favorite scenes, Junior Soprano, Tony's uncle (played by the great Dominic Chianese) decides to announce this in front of his family at the dinner table. This is the second time Junior had said this in front of people. Tony recalls, when he was a kid, his uncle used to tell his girl cousins the same thing which he admits to Junior was very hurtful. Tony screams at him, "It's undermining, and that's exactly what I teach my kids Not To Do! So I don't want to hear it again! End of Subject!" he shouts, raising his arm swiftly in an Italian gesture. I am assuming suffering from early signs of dementia, Junior again in conversation repeats the same phrase. Tony blows up, slams his fork down on the table, and announces he is leaving with A.J. Here is a mob boss tough as nails unraveled by the confirmation that his uncle, whom he loves, never thought he was a good enough athlete in high school. Case in point: People often say, "We spend all of our adulthood getting over our childhood." I guess Tony Soprano was no exception.

My brother tried so hard to get me to live the life he thought I should be living. At the end of the day, he loved me, and he wanted all of us to be happy. In reality, Bill was always just as sweet as the character Bobby Baccalieri (Steve Schirripa) on *The Sopranos*, who also happens to be one of my favorites. Bill even tried to set me up with a nice guy from his office early on.

I, on the other hand, liked to live outside the box with no real plan. Keeping my depression under control by working in an environment that was good for me was my main concern.

Big Dog, like my wonderful late father before him, planned for his future early on by putting money aside for retirement. It served both of them well because, in the corporate world, if you died, your job position would be listed before your obituary.

My youngest brother told his company he was sick. The next day, he walked into work to find someone sitting at his desk. He was told to teach him his job. What his company did to him keeps me up some nights. Even his colleagues stuck up for him. I expect nothing less from corporate America. But my little brother worked for a *life insurance company*. Take a bow. I wonder how these people sleep at night. My brother was up many nights suffering, and they just added to his pain.

I had owned several birds. Big Dog often said, "Get rid of those birds! A guy is going to see an unmarried single woman with all those birds and leave skid marks!"

Because I had no real retirement plan, he often jokingly told me that I was going to end up like the old lady from *Mary Poppins* who fed the birds in the park. I told him to be sure he put a coin in my jar as he passed. We both laughed but some of the things he said did worry me a little. Bill didn't understand my depression and how it limited me throughout the years. I had a comfort zone, and that's where I wanted to stay.

When I got a cat, I thought he was seriously going to cry. "You *got* a *cat!*" He was truly upset. "A guy is going to take one look at all those birds and that cat and run for the hills, I'm telling you. You never *listen* to me!" He shook his head and walked away. I guess the cat was a deal breaker. For him, an older woman with birds and now a cat—in his mind, if there had ever been a minute chance of me finding someone at my age, I had just blown it.

So Big Dog tried hard to keep the family on the right track. My late father would have been so proud of how he took care of all of us, especially my mother.

"Listen and obey!" he would say jokingly. We all laughed at that, but at the end of the day, he was usually right.

Like my father, Bill was like a big teddy bear until you pushed him too far. He had a presence like Tony Soprano too, and when he was angry was just as scary. He was the one we called in a crisis— and he showed up every time. He'd say, "You're killing me" in response to the constant bail-out situations that would occur. He'd have loved to see me settled down with a nice guy and a stable career. It just wasn't in the cards.

Years later I often told family members and friends that I was going to write a book and then have it developed into a movie. After seeing Robert DeNiro's performance in *Silver Linings Playbook*, which I thought was brilliant, I thought he would be perfect to play Big Dog.

"Don, you know you keep telling people that you're going to make a movie, and you want *Robert De Niro to play me?* You have to hear the way you sound when you talk like this. What I'm saying, not to hurt your feelings, but you do sound a little on the strange side. I'm just saying. . . ."

"You'll see, Bill."

4

NINETY-NINE PERCENT

"Hi, John. I'm a friend of your sister Veronica. She told me that you cast for the background of the Sopranos. Is that true?"

"Yes, that is correct, the Sopranos and a lot of other TV shows and movies. Are you available to come in for an interview today around three o'clock?"

"That would be great! Can I have the address?" I asked, scrambling in my pocketbook for an old envelope and something to write with.

I arrived to find a charming yet little hole-in-the-wall agency with many black-and-white portraits covering all the reception-room walls. The subjects were of different ages, races, shapes, and sizes. I guess it would make sense, because, when you watch movies and TV, people in the background must look real. We don't have gorgeous movie stars walking around us all the time, so to be an extra there is no set criteria.

As I was studying the pictures, I heard a door open and turned around to see an attractive man enter: brown hair, slightly long in the back, and a V-shaped body. Trailing behind him was a cute guy, a little older, with a teddy bear look—all smiles.

"Hi, I'm John, and this is Jim. Come in and have a seat."

We did, and I sat down. John said that Jim would go over what the membership included. I told them my sorry tale of missing my chance to meet James Gandolfini. They were trying to get me to join their agency, so hearing about this little obsession of mine was a definite plus for a potential sale.

They had an act going on between them. I wouldn't say good-cop, bad-cop—it was more businessman and cheerleader. Jim started to explain the cost, and what was included. He explained that an ex-television actor would give me eight professional acting classes, all included. As soon as he was done saying that, John passed the open door, stuck his head in, and said, "Oh, yeah, the acting classes are great! This guy is a professional actor. You'll love it! We do a show at the end of the classes of a scene that you'll learn. It's really great!"

Jim added that a professional photographer would take head shots of me in three different outfits. We would get to pick the one we liked, and a hundred copies would be made. The agency would give fifty to me and keep fifty to use in applying for jobs. They'd also keep a digital copy on the computer to send out to ads who wanted a specific look. They'd get a percentage of what you earned on every job they sent you out on.

It all sounded great to me, but I'd heard that a lot of such agencies were scams, especially if they asked you for money, so I was a little wary.

John popped in again and said, "The head shots come out great! We send them out to get jobs for you and the photographer is right next door."

They told me how much it would cost but said that, if I joined at that moment, they would take off a hundred dollars.

It was still steep. I had just climbed out of the worst pre-partum depression and still wasn't fully recovered. I had found out that Billy had bought a quarter-million-dollar house and moved in with a girl and her two kids. I was beyond crushed. The thought of it sickened me. I needed a diversion, something else to put my mind on, and I was thinking this could be it. "What do you say, Don?" John concluded. "It's a great opportunity. Come on, I'm telling you, you won't regret it. . .but you have to decide now, if you want the discount."

"How do I know you're not ripping me off?"

"How can I rip you off? You know my *sister*."

Actually, I had just met Veronica that day, but *he* didn't know that.... "John, if I join, you have to promise me one hundred percent that you will get me on *The Sopranos*. I really want that picture with James Gandolfini."

He looked at me, paused for a second, and said, "I can't promise you one hundred percent that I can get you on *The Sopranos*."

I said, "Then what percentage can you promise me?"

He said, "I promise you ninety-nine percent. . .if you join *today*. . .that I'll get you on *The Sopranos*."

That was good enough for me. I took some cash from my pocketbook along with two credit cards. All I kept thinking was that, if my family knew how much I was spending, considering I'd lost my job and my apartment due to my breakdown, it wouldn't go over well. It didn't stop me. Something told me to do it, so I did.

I walked out of there thinking, *I just got totally ripped off. What am I, stupid?*

John had told me to make sure I kept my phone nearby in case a job came in. I just yessed him to death, thinking I'd probably never hear from him again.

Oprah Winfrey said, "Listen to your whispers."

I have had a lot of them in my life. Sometimes they tell me to do things or go places outside my comfort zone, and I ask myself, "Why am I *doing* this?" Later, I discover the reason. It always leads me to a good person or place. I joined the agency on a whim, using money I didn't have, but I followed my gut feeling. I decided not to worry, keep it to myself, and put it out of my mind. . .for now.

5

DANA

"H I, DANA, IT'S ME." Dana is my best friend. We have been friends since high school. She was a freshman, and I a junior. I remember her always coming up to our lunch table to ask me if she could borrow a couple of bucks. I gave them to her. She never forgot that kindness and insisted on treating me to a lot of things throughout the years. Dana was the kind of person who would give you the shirt off her back.

"What's up?" she asked. "I can't talk long—I have to do a stress test. What's the matter?" Her accent was a little thicker than *typical* Jersey; it was more like *North Bergen*, New Jersey, if you're familiar. That's where she's originally from. She actually had it worse than I did as far as bullying went. To avoid getting beat up, the school would let her out ten minutes early to give her a head start home.

I said, laughing, "Why do you always think something's the matter when I call?... I saw Billy in court today."

Dana suffered the same bouts of anxiety and depression I did over the years. We understood each other. Unless you have experienced these things, it is very hard to relate or understand what a person is going through. I called her when I was at a low, and vice versa. We knew what to say to each other if and when a dark day overshadowed us.

Dana often said, "Don't give *in* to it. You can't give *in* to it."

And I have played her words back in my head on all sorts of occasions, and then was able to slowly inch my way off the couch and rejoin the living.

When Dana started nursing school, she was a little mischievous. A teacher went so far as to tell her she wasn't going to amount to anything. Devastated over a breakup, Dana briefly dropped out. She eventually found the strength to go back and finish, determined to prove the teacher wrong. She went all the way with her education, making the dean's list more than once. She's running a cardiac rehab now and teaches as well. I have to say, the way she cares for her patients is a close second to Mother Theresa—no exaggeration.

She's like that when her friends and family need her as well. People like Dana do not come around too often. I'm very lucky to have her as a friend.

We've gone out together about a million times over the years. We've had the craziest, most memorable times. She's listened to me talk about Billy over and over, more times than I think she cared to, but that's what good friends do. She could never understand how, after all that had happened, I could still have feelings for him, but she was still there for me regardless.

During my pregnancy, I couldn't see or speak to anyone, I was so distraught. Regardless of her current back pain, Dana announced she was coming over to paint an old little room in my mother's house meant for the baby. I reluctantly agreed. I watched her paint the whole room by herself from my bedroom door. I think it was her way of trying to ease my pain the only way she knew how.

I had no idea she would play such a big part in my existence today. One day, Dana made a hard choice and did what she had to do. . .to ultimately save my life.

6

UNCLE LEO

Uncle Leo is not actually my uncle through blood. He's been best friends with my dad since grade school. We grew up with his kids and spent a lot of time with him and his family. He walks every day, drinks tap water, and has never gone to a doctor. At seventy-eight, he's doing great.

Growing up, I'd hear him say in a Penny Marshall-type voice, "They are *poisoning* us with the food. . .all the chemicals they're adding."

Yeah, yeah, Uncle Leo, I thought when I heard it as a kid. "The Government this, the Government that."

I realize now that maybe I should have listened more to Uncle Leo. A lot of what he used to say was not too far off. He's been right about a lot of things.

His personality is a cross between Woody Allen and Larry David (as portrayed in most of their work). One of these great actors would be perfect to play him in my movie.

Their onscreen presence tends to be over-analytical; like them, my uncle is also bothered by the little annoyances in life. If you got into a discussion with him about anything he felt strongly about, he'd argue the point until he had convinced you that he was...well, *basically* right.

My dad and he talked every day on the phone, especially when they grew older. After my dear father passed, I started to call Uncle Leo. I don't know if I was doing it more for him or myself. Talking to my father's best friend made me feel closer to my dad. I enjoyed our discussions, too. I know my uncle misses my father. I miss him as well. He needed him, considering he lost several people close to him in a short period of time—his wife, mother, grandson, my brother (his Godson), and his nephew, all within about five years.

"Everyone has moved on from the bereavement group. They're going on with their lives. It's not working for me," he says.

"Uncle Leo, they've had only one person die. You've had a *rainfall*...how can you compare?"

"Yeah. I guess."

I really wish my dad could have been here for him. My uncle says my father's visited him in a dream on more than one occasion. The last time he dreamt about him, he says, my father told him, "I have to go, and I won't be back for a while." It was the last time he saw him.

I hope one day Dad finds his way into one of my dreams—I would really love to see him again.

7

KAREN

I HAVE GONE TO A FEW THERAPISTS in my life, mostly in my younger years. I have not found them to be much help. They were nice enough but the way I see it, how are you going to recover from a war if you are still in the line of fire every day?

As I grew older, around my early thirties, I once again tried to seek help for my depression. I called my provider and wrote down some numbers. The therapists who called back sounded cold and unfeeling. I started seeing one anyway; she looked more depressed than I was. I felt that she was just going through the motions.

Then I came down with a bad flu and missed a session or two. She didn't even call to see what had happened to me. I never went back.

I decided to call a woman, who got back to me late. She was the only one who asked me how I was doing, which was a definite plus. I knew right away from the kindness in her voice that I should see her. She sounded very professional—one of the few therapists who didn't use the four words the rest of them reached for when you ask for advice, which are, "What do you think?"

I went to meet Karen at the office in her beautiful home. She was an attractive woman, very well dressed in a suit jacket, skirt, and high heels. Every time I saw her, she was dressed up. Her makeup was perfect, jewelry and her strawberry red hair just so. She reminded me a little of Dr. Melfi the way she would sit and cross her legs and ask questions that maybe sometimes you didn't want to answer. The goal was trying to get to the root of the problem; for me it was a number of things—not seeing the warning signs when it came to relationships, staying in them too long, and, eventually, being treated badly.

"Look for the warning signs," Karen would say. "You have to take care of yourself. If you see them, get out of there. Don't wait until you're hooked. If they're treating you badly now, it will never get better."

Like Dr. Melfi, Karen thought certain things or situations might trigger a relapse with depression or a drastic reaction. Not paying attention to the warning signs was my biggest problem; it would cause old wounds to resurface and ultimately put me in a bad place.

Tony Soprano's triggers can also be traced back to long ago. According to Dr. Melfi, an event from Tony's childhood might be linked to one of the causes of his panic attacks. In one of his sessions, Tony told Dr. Melfi about an incident when he was eleven years old. He saw his father cut off a man's pinky in the back of his butcher shop. Later that day, he saw his mother cooking up a piece of meat from that very same place while flirting with his father in a sexual manner. "The lady loves her meat," his father said.

Witnessing his mother turned on by his father's violent ways, young Tony stares at the meat cooking and falls to the floor. Dr. Melfi believes meat, his parents' sexuality, and his panic attacks are somehow connected. This wouldn't be the first time Tony has this reaction to meat. I think Dr. Melfi is on to something.

Childhood traumas have a way of catching up to you in your adult life. If not treated, people might try to self-medicate. This will only add to your problem's. I suggest you seek help and hopefully end up in a room with someone as good as Karen or if you are really lucky . . . Dr. Melfi.

8

TAKE TWO

THE YEARS MARCHED ON QUICKLY in my life. I seemed to go through stages much later than most. Marriage was not a priority. Friends in my circle had already found their mates. The few men I picked, I knew deep down, long term, would have been a disaster. I spent most of my free time with children. By now, Gina and Noah were married. I grew close to their kids as well as my own nieces and nephews. The unconditional love I received from them cured whatever life threw at me. It also kept my depression in check—for the most part.

Children have always been my saving grace. In sixth grade, to avoid harassment on the playground, they had put me in the kindergarten class to help the teacher. It was a Godsend—avoiding the lunchroom, and the free time after, like an early Christmas gift.

It worked out well until the kids started liking me more than the teacher. Then, without explanation, I was sent back to the wolves. During our sixth-grade graduation ceremony, none of my peers clapped for me when I went up to receive my paper diploma. But to my surprise, when I looked down at the very front row, I saw about twenty adorable faces with wide smiles cheering and clapping. That's a very special memory. Children have brought me nothing but joy.

I didn't think I would ever have a child of my own. As I got older, I refused to settle for just anyone. I was waiting for that "Great Love" that I thought would someday find me.

I was content being alone. I didn't want to be attached to anyone. After many years, I managed to move out of my parents' house and get a place of my own. I did get lonely at times, but I had a great group of friends, so the tradeoff was worth it.

I wanted to shed some extra pounds I'd put on from the antidepressants I was taking. I knew I'd have to slowly ween myself off them. The last time I tried had been a nightmare. But, I thought, this time I was exercising and feeling good about myself with no real stresses, so I decided to try it once again.

I went to a lot of Gina and Noah's family functions but made a point of avoiding any that Billy might attend—one ghost from my past I did not want to see. I heard through the grapevine that he was having marital troubles, but I didn't give it a second thought.

Three months later, I heard Noah's older brother Tony and his girlfriend had just split, and that he was in bad shape. His mother, Roe, was trying to get him to go out so he could get his mind off the situation and thought it was a good idea for us to get together.

I knew it wasn't; we'd known each other for years, and it would definitely be a rebound. He was a great guy, more like Noah, but Karen's warnings started playing in my head, so I avoided the prospect. He went on to meet a nice woman and is happy to this day. Go figure. I guess the rebound curse did not apply for him, but I'm glad it worked out.

Then Gina called me one night. She wanted to go out on the town for old time's sake. I think she wanted to relive our club days. We wound up at a neighborhood Knights of Columbus. When we walked in, we knew just about everybody. Coming from a small town, it wasn't a surprise. Gina greeted everyone with a smile as we made our way to the bar to get a drink. At the far end of it—I couldn't believe my eyes—was Billy, sitting by himself.

"Billy's here," she said, and made her way towards him.

I followed her, with no time for it to register. I hadn't seen him in years.

"Hi, Billy! What are *you* doing here?" Gina asked as she leaned over and kissed him on the cheek.

"Hi, Billy," I said. "How you doing?"

"Okay, I guess. Could be better. How about you? . . . It's been awhile," he added, looking into my eyes with a half-smile on his face.

Gina took over the conversation until she was called away by a friend. I sat down next to him. He told me he'd been out of his house for a couple of months. He thought his wife of fifteen years was cheating on him. He looked very upset. I should have realized that there were two sides to every story. I guess, at the time, I had no reason to doubt him.

We all hung out for a while, drinking and catching up. It was nice to feel comfortable with him for a change. I was not the shy girl he had once known. He asked me if I wanted to go out sometime. I had no interest, and I told myself, there *is no way I'm getting in the middle of this scenario. It has disaster written all over it.* I could see Karen's face pop up in this little bubble, shaking her head from side to side.

The other side of my brain, needless to say, tried to rationalize it: *It worked out for his brother Tony when he was on the rebound. Life is full of chances.*

Lucille Ball once said, "I'd rather regret the things I've done than regret the things I haven't done." Hmm. . .I've always loved Lucy.

He *had* been separated for months and was out of his house. I didn't want to hurt his feelings because he was already feeling low. I told him that I would love to go out with him, but that he needed to figure out where he was going with his relationship. When and if he ever filed for divorce, we could go out.

I didn't think for a minute that he'd go through with it. Men never do, especially if they have a lot to lose. He had money, property, and a successful business. For once in my life, I was going to be smart. I guess all that time in therapy was finally paying off. He agreed, but we still exchanged numbers. I told him he could call me if he needed someone to talk to. I figured, what harm could that do?

We spoke a couple of times the next week. Slowly the feelings I had for him so long ago started to resurface. Billy seemed to have changed over the years. He was no longer a kid out for himself. He was a man and a hands-on father to his kids. I heard he'd set up trust funds for them and become a coach for their sporting events. They loved him—a successful, self-made businessman who started with nothing. I admired that, especially the kind of father he turned out to be. I was falling in love with him all over again.

Then came the day when he told me he was filing for divorce...and he did.

The next night I asked him to come over. Nervous and excited at the same time, I was glad I had bought some wine. I was still trying to process what was happening.

The doorbell rang, and there he was. He came in and sat down. We started joking and laughing and having a good time. He told me how glad he was to see me again. We talked about our first date and all the old times with Noah and Gina.

Hours flew by. It got really late—about three o'clock in the morning. He looked at me and in a shaky voice asked, "Can I just give you a kiss?"

I nodded, and he leaned in with his full lips and began to kiss me slowly and gently. We looked at each other for a moment and started kissing again, longer. He was very respectful. My body language was telling him to go further, but I could tell he was holding back. I knew he didn't want me to think he was the same as he'd been years before.

I put my hands up his shirt and rubbed my hands across

his chest. I led his hand under my shirt to my breast to let him know it was okay. He started caressing me, feeling me, getting me so aroused. For a moment, I was seventeen again, underwear soaked and hot with desire...for him.

The only difference between then and now was that this time I was not going to stop him. We had waited long enough. I wanted his body in mine, thrusting me, kissing me, everything I had been afraid to do years before.

He took my hand, and we went into the bedroom; we couldn't keep our hands off each other. He took his time. We took our time. I got lost in his body, lost in a daze...and then I felt this sharp feeling of pleasure and let out a loud moan—he was inside me.

9

WHERE WERE YOU?

OH, THERE'S MY PHONE. Finally, I see it way under the seat. I couldn't find it for a couple of days. I tried calling it, but the volume was off. It is impossible to find your phone when that happens. I thought I had lost it for good. Plugging it into the charger, I turn it on to find I have five missed calls from John. It's only been a couple of days since I left him—what could he possibly want? I quickly call him back. "Hi. You called?"

"Where *were* you? I've been calling you for two days, and it went right to voicemail. I had a job for you, a television show called *The Black Donnelly*. I told you to keep your phone with you."

"Sorry, John. I just found the phone, the volume was off. Is it too late?"

"Yep, sorry. I had to call someone else. Next time, keep your phone with you. Talk to you later. Bye."

I'm shocked; I didn't know he would call so fast or even

call at all for that matter. Oh, damn, a TV show—that would have been cool.

From that day on, I kept my phone charged and right by my side. A couple days later, John calls again. "Hey, Don, I have a job for you...well, actually, for your car. Are you interested?"

"Really? What is it?"

"Will Smith is making a movie called *I Am Legend*, and they need all types of cars in a scene. New York City is supposed to look deserted or something because of an alien virus, I think, or something like that."

"Yeah, sure. I'll do it."

I write down all the information. I have to report to New York City at 4:00 a.m. with my car. I'm so bad with directions, but the opportunity to be part of a movie with Will Smith, even if it's just my car, makes my fears take a back seat to my determination. Where there's a will, there's a way—no pun intended.

My father stays on the phone with me and gave me step-by-step directions so I will get there alright, this is before all these GPS devices. My dad's the best.

We all have to park our cars is disarray on one of the streets in Manhattan. There are large trucks in the mix as well. While we all wait in our cars, someone was putting mud and dust all over all them. I guess they do it to make it look like a lot of time has passed.

I see everyone start to get out of their cars and trucks. I get out as well and follow them over to a group of other extras. Is Will Smith here? I wonder. I hope so; that would be cool.

As we're standing there talking and taking it all in, we hear a speeding racecar. We turn to see a bright red sports car, with a double white stripe down the middle, speeding down the road past us.

"Is it Will?" we all ask each other.

"Nope, just a stunt double," says some guy standing next to us.

It would have been nice, but watching the scene was still exciting. Then we hear a man yelling loudly at someone. Who's that? What happened? Apparently, while shooting the scene, someone forgot to put the stunt "artificial dog" that was supposed to be riding with Will in the car. So they have to reshoot the scene. The director is not happy.

On my way back to New Jersey, I can't believe where I just was. I loved it. It took my mind off my severed heart and made me feel alive again. John was telling me the truth. If he got me on this set, there is a strong possibility that just maybe I could make it to The Sopranos. Who knows? Only time will tell. In twenty minutes, I'm over the bridge and back in Jersey, my muddy car and I, waiting to share my excitement.

10

WILL SMITH

LET ME TELL YOU, I absolutely love this guy. I knew he would be genuine and kind to his fans. There are actors I've come across who cannot be bothered to show any appreciation for us poor non-union extras. We're making less than a hundred dollars to stand, run, sit, or whatever else we're required to do for however long. But it was worth it standing out in the cold making the movie *I Am Legend* with Will Smith.

I was at the agency one night enjoying my acting class when John walked in. He wanted to see if any of us wanted to be in the movie. I volunteered, as did some of my new friends from the agency. Natasha, a fiery red-haired Russian, Dustin, Eric, and my acting partner Toni Ann were all on board.

John pulled me aside and told me that it might be pretty rough and was I sure I wanted to do it. It was going to be a six-night shoot outdoors, near the Brooklyn Bridge, and the weather was going to be brutal. It *was* January, but I knew it was an opportunity I couldn't pass up, so I told him I was in. I couldn't wait to be a part of it.

The movie was based on a 1954 novel by Richard Matheson. Its premise concerns a brilliant scientist, Robert Neville (whom Will Smith would play), who seemed to be the only survivor of a manmade virus. He is alone in New York City with ex-humans who have been transformed into bloodthirsty mutants. He works on finding a cure while fighting extreme loneliness—and scary zombies whenever the sun goes down.

I was so excited. My acting friends had rented a motel together around the corner for the six nights so they wouldn't have to go back and forth to Jersey. I would have loved to join them, but I wanted to be home at night to see my daughter. I was living with my parents then, and my mom didn't mind taking care of her. She'd started to see a living spark reignite in me, and if this was what it took, she was all for it.

Okay, here we are in freezing weather at a port below the Brooklyn Bridge. Wardrobe instructions were simply to dress very warm and have a rolling suitcase. I arrive to see hundreds of people in several large tents. I am with the non-union extras; there was another area for union members. I found my friends from the agency, and we all sat at one table.

I later learned that the scenes we shot by the Brooklyn Bridge, which took six nights, cost over five million bucks to shoot. The producers needed approval from fourteen different government agencies. The scene required a crew of two hundred and fifty plus hundreds of extras, including a hundred and sixty National Guard troops in full combat gear.

Night is falling. We are called outside. There are tons of people. We are instructed to run toward the bridge in a panic. My friend Marina and I are hanging together the first night.

Ready...*action!* We start running with our suitcases, dodging and weaving around a horde of other people. I can't even describe how surreal it feels. *I am part of a major motion picture. How did I get here?*

I spot a military car trying to get through the crowd. It's Will Smith's character trying to get to the port to get his movie family out of New York via helicopter. But he can't get through. He jumps out and runs around the car to grab his little girl (played by his actual daughter Willow Smith). Holding her, with his wife in tow, he rushes through the crowd towards the pier.

"*Cut!*" the director yells. "Everyone back to your mark."

"*Action!*" he soon shouts, and we run as fast as we can again, in a panic, trying to get to the port.

We must have done this thirty times, no kidding. Marina hurt her leg at one point and had to drop out of the movie. I, on the other hand, tried to run fast enough from my mark to get to the place where Wil Smith was walking around the car, so I could be in the movie.

"*Action!*"

There I go, running up the street, dodging and weaving, trying to time it right to where Will is walking around the car. I see the car...did I miss him? Then, *boom!* I didn't miss him—I crash hard, at full speed, right into his chest.

It was like hitting a brick wall. I don't fall, but my suitcase flies out of my hand, and I lose my footing a little. Hey—maybe that'll make the movie. I couldn't wait to tell everyone I crashed into Will Smith. I'm such a weirdo.

As the days went on, the excitement was indescribable. I would be inches away from Will in his military suit, holding his real daughter Willow with her red coat on. *Am I seeing this?* I asked myself more than once. At one point, I looked at her, smiled, and waved. She smiled back. Later, I spotted her red coat again, but I had to look twice, because her face looked different, a lot older. *Am I seeing things?* I wondered. It turned out she was a little person with the same coat and a wig. It was way too cold for Willow to be out there that long.

I met three young Asian girls on the bridge. I still have their picture. I won't forget them, they were so sweet. We hung out night after night. I kept a lot of treats in my suitcase to give the young kids if they were hungry. It was freezing, so I'd get body warmers to put under my clothes and in my shoes. The union extras had a heated tent close to production. Our tent was farther away. Being part of SAG definitely has its perks. I will not soon forget Natasha shouting to the crowd, in her unmistakably Russian accent, "I don't need Union. . .I was in Soviet Union. Non-union is *best!*"

I heard someone screaming and tried to move closer to see what was going on. It was an actress playing her part for the movie. She was flipping out because she could not leave with her children. They could see whether you were infected by the virus by checking your eyes. Natasha was so excited that they'd chosen her to be checked, which might possibly lead her to being in the film. It turned out to be a letdown, because it somehow fell by the wayside. I felt really bad for her. Her career as an extra flourished subsequently regardless—she's been in dozens of films and shows. The one I saw her in was a TV series, with Harvey Keitel, called *Life on Mars*. Natasha was to play a dead person lying on the ground with Keitel standing over her, music blaring, when suddenly a tiny helicopter came flying slowly out of her ear. You can't make this stuff up. I was so excited for her, especially since she was in the scene with Harvey Keitel. He is one of the great actors of our time— who, by the way, has excellent taste in women. After all, he had a long-term serious relationship with Dr. Melfi (Lorraine Bracco). He was very blessed.

The director of *I Am Legend* told us that, in the film, the bridge was going to blow up. On his cue, we would all have to scream and react. We did it several times. Of course, the bridge wouldn't really blow up, we'd just have to pretend it did. This is going to be fun, I thought. I love it!

"*Action!*" He gave us the cue, and we all screamed, covering our faces and expressing looks of horror. We did it many times. It *was* so much fun.

Over his microphone, he said, "Okay, that was great. Now we are going to do it again, and this time I want you to *pantomime*. Action!"

He gave us the cue when the bridge blew up. Everyone screamed. I was experimenting with my acting skills, so this time I reacted differently, a little more hysterically.

"*Cut!*" the director yelled. "Again! But I want you *pantomime!*"

We all screamed and reacted and did our best to please him, but he began to get frustrated. Someone must have told him that we didn't know what pantomiming was. He became apologetic and told us it just meant reacting to something without sound. We finally did it the correct way. Having hundreds of people react to a bridge that wasn't really blowing up without a sound was *wonderfully* surreal.

It was getting brutal out there in the January cold, and a lot of people dropped out. I was determined to make it the full six days. Towards the end, some would sneak back to the hotel and warm up a little, and then return, hoping nobody would notice. On one of the last days, I decided to do the same. When I arrived, I got a phone call from my friend. "Don, where *are* you? Will Smith is *singing to the crowd*. He's doing his rap songs. Hurry up, you're going to miss it!" Of *course*, I thought—the minute I leave.

The next day, before nightfall and the start of filming, my friend and I happened to see Will walking on the street towards his trailer.

I said, "Hi, Will, can I take a picture?" He turned around and posed with a big friendly smile on his face.

My camera was jammed. "Oh! Wait, Will, my camera jammed."

He stepped back and gladly posed for another one. I didn't get to see him sing and the picture didn't come out, but it was an amazing experience I won't soon forget. I knew Will Smith would be great in person.

Having an amazing, talented wife like Jada Pinkette Smith by his side of course contributes to the great man he is today. Her Red round table and her fearless honesty about her own life has helped so many people including myself.

Will Smith is an outstanding actor and, more importantly, he has a warm heart and a kind soul.

11

RISE AND SHINE

WHEN MY EYES OPENED the morning after I first slept with Billy, the sun was glaring into my bedroom window. I felt the taste of wine still in my mouth, and it suddenly hit me what had occurred the night before. I saw that I was alone in the bed and thought, where is he? I knew he'd slept over. *Did he leave? . . .*

What was that? I heard something in the other room; it must be him. This is so embarrassing, I immediately thought. What am I going to say? How is he going to act? . . . *Here he comes! Make believe you're sleeping.*

I heard him come in. He sat on the edge of the bed and kissed me gently on the cheek.

"Good morning," I said, opening my eyes slowly as if I had just woken up.

"Good morning. I had such a great time last night," he said softly as he slowly stroked my hair.

"I did, too."

"I have to go to work now, but I'd like to take you out to dinner tonight if that's okay with you."

He looked right into my eyes; we stared at each other for a moment, then kissed gently on the lips. I got up and followed him to the door. He told me he would call me later so we could make plans for that night. He left then, and from that moment on, I couldn't get him out of my mind.

That night, he picked me up and took me to a fancy restaurant. We had a great time talking and laughing. We were so *comfortable* with each other. Maybe this is what I was missing in my life, I thought. Had it taken all those years to finally bring us together? It was a little early to speculate, but all I knew was that, when I was with him, I felt like I was home. That's what people say when they feel that's where they belong. That's the feeling I got when I was with Billy.

He came back to my apartment that night and never left. We wanted to be together all the time, so he was living with me. Before he left in the mornings, he wrote me love notes. I would shop for all the clothes that I knew he loved. Stretch pants were his favorite.

Billy Loved a woman who could cook, too. I did the best I could, but I was no Martha Stewart. I almost started a grease fire making filet mignon one night. The whole apartment was filled with smoke, and the fire alarm went off and kept blaring. Billy walked in right at that moment. I was so embarrassed. He quickly shut off the alarm, opened the windows and went to get my little fan from my storage area. Seeing the sad look on my face, he couldn't help but to release his signature laugh, reach over, hug me, and say, "Oh, come on...you'll get better."

He did everything for me. We made love every night. After, I fell asleep on his chest with his arms around me. It was just as it had been so many years before—just where I wanted to be. I guessed it was what real love felt like. I couldn't say, in my life, that I'd ever felt that way before. Was it meant to be—fate—or just too good to be true?

Maybe all of the above.

12

LAW AND ORDER SVU

EARLIER, JOHN WAS CALLING ME at least three times a week. I was also attending the acting class the agency provided, which turned out to be one of the best things I ever did for myself. Hairdressing helped me become more confident and outgoing, but after that acting class, I could get up in front of any number of people, in any situation, and speak. I didn't even think twice about it. I had come a long way from the shy, quiet, insecure girl I had been. I was confident, outgoing, and fearless; it was the perfect diversion from the devastation I had suffered. I'd dreamed forever of being in the entertainment industry in some way, and it couldn't have come at a better time.

"Don, we put you down for *Law and Order: SVU* tomorrow, okay?"

"*Really?* Thanks, John! I love that show!"

"You're going to be playing a prisoner. It's taking place in a real prison. A few other women are going, so you guys can share a ride. They'll be supplying the wardrobe. Check in time is 6:00 a.m. Don't be late and have fun.

"Thanks, John, I will."

I got off the phone and called my parents. They were going to flip. They watched that show all the time. I couldn't wait.

I DROVE MY OWN CAR to the prison with one of my extra friends. We had to go through security and were told where the prohibited areas were. We were led to the waiting area, where a pile of orange jumpsuits awaited us. Cool, I thought. This is going to be fun.

It didn't surprise me that, when I got there, I found yet another group of people that were anything but ordinary. People who work as extras can range from the retired and financially free to aspiring actors, slightly strange, and sometimes, yes, even the homeless.

I came across two girls who were quite interesting. One was a little tough-looking, about five feet five and of medium build, all smiles and very serious about her craft. While we were waiting to be called, she asked me to run a couple of lines with her for a play she was doing. I was glad to do it. I read my part the best I could, considering that the scene was very emotional. When her part came up, which called for extreme sadness, she started to cry as she read her lines. With real tears flowing, eventually she started wailing with grief. All the attention in the room was on us. It was like the orgasm scene in the *When Harry Met Sally*. I just stood there and couldn't believe the transformation. What a surprise...but meeting extras is often full of surprises.

The other girl I met told me she was a stunt woman. At some point, a guard was supposed to throw her across a table. I guess she was paid a little extra for that. I was intrigued by her career choice. She wasn't treated any different than the rest of us. We were all were in the same room, just waiting for the call. I put a bandana around my head so I would appear tougher. I couldn't wait to get started and see all the stars.

We are going to have a prison riot of some sort. In the episode at hand, Mariska Hargitay, who plays Detective Olivia Benson, goes undercover as one of the prisoners. She is trying to expose a guard who is raping and threatening female prisoners.

They started calling out everyone in groups. I was in one of the last. I didn't want to miss the opportunity to be on the episode, so when the third group was called, I waited until they left, then slipped away, following them down in the elevator. I entered the room to see Mariska Hargitay in the middle of demonstrating how to put handcuffs on. She was joking about how long she had been a cop. She didn't have any makeup on, but she looked just as beautiful.

She was different from a lot of the other celebrities I've come across. She didn't treat extras like wallpaper. She made eye contact and acted as if we were a team. When you worked with her, she made you feel just as important as any other actor on the show. Special instructions hadn't been left for us not to speak to her. If they had, we would have heard about it. Her mother, who was Hollywood royalty, would have been proud of the person she turned out to be.

Okay, it's time to shoot. They want to give shots to all the prisoners, because there is an STD going around. Mariska's character wants to know why. All the prisoners start asking why. Things start getting out of hand.

Some girl is leaning on my back.

We are all shouting, "What's going on? We have a right to know."

The riot starts, and an alarm starts blaring. The guards come in with their clubs.

Everyone starts screaming. The excitement explodes! Then the guard grabs the stunt woman and just flings her across the table. Another guard hit another girl in the back with his club. She must be another stunt woman. This is *awesome!*

In the next scene, we all had to get on our knees against the wall, hands behind our heads. One elderly extra lost her balance and fell but got up and quickly and assumed the position.

Mariska Hargitay complimented us all on what a great job we had done.

We hadn't eaten lunch, so it was time for a break. I couldn't believe it, but our own little riot broke out on the long lunch line. I think somebody tried to cut in. I'd never seen that behavior before on the job. Maybe it was the atmosphere and the orange jumpsuits. I assure you, after spending a day at a prison and a little time locked in a cell (which I had done on the regular *Law and Order*), you *never* want to end up in jail for any length of time. Then it was time to go, so we all signed out and returned the orange attire. We couldn't help but talk about the excitement of the day.

I was about to leave when I felt a desire to walk up to Mariska Hargitay and mention that both our children were named one of the months of the year. I was a little nervous but decided to do it. I saw her talking to someone. When she saw me standing there, she held one finger up to the person and, with a big smile, said, "Hi."

When she turned to me again, I said, "Hi, Mariska, I just wanted to show you a picture of my daughter. Your son, who's the same age, is named a month of the year, and so is she."

She looked at the picture and told me how cute she was. I thanked her and was on my way.

When I saw the episode, if you blinked, you would miss me and my bandana. What I did see was all those nice people, all characters unique in their own way, that I had spent the day with. And a great day it was.

13

SELECTIVE HEARING

Things with Billy couldn't have been better. He even gave me my own little walkie-talkie, so that he could contact me no matter where I was. Billy had a thriving business and earned a good living. He no longer had to do the dirty work himself; he was the boss and had his workers do it for him.

Money seemed to be no object to him either then. Once very conservative, I guess he thought he had worked hard enough and was going to splurge a little. He bought a brand-new Mustang, which I thought was a good start. We had a blast going places in that car. I was the only one he would let drive it for any length of time; naturally, that made me feel special. I mean, a man and his car are a very sacred thing. Often cars would pull up alongside us, revving their engines, wanting to race.

I'd say, "No, don't do it, Billy!"

But he'd be all for it. He'd look at me, smile mischievously, and step on the gas.

"Billy, *stop! Stop!* Let me out!"

Eventually, he'd slow down, seeing how terrified I was. "I'm sorry, I'm sorry," he'd say as he put his hand on mine.

I HAD HEARD, WHEN BILLY WAS SEPARATED, something about him using. . .but I had shrugged it off. I figured maybe he was just dabbling in it recreationally because of the separation. I think we had both sampled some in our younger years but seen what had happened to other people and in time abstained. I didn't think that he would risk all his sweat and tears over the years building his business just to throw it away. People who start using often feel that it will never happen to them, or that they can somehow keep it under control. I'm here to tell you. . .wrong and wrong.

If you make the conscious decision to start using drugs, from then on, you risk your sense of control, especially if you're vulnerable. I'm sure you've heard of a "functioning alcoholic." But you rarely hear of a functioning drug addict. If there are any, they most likely have an enabler. Eventually the walls will—not might, *will*—come crashing down.

I came home one morning to find the light blinking on my answering machine. It's probably Billy, I told myself. He always leaves a nice message. *Hi, Don,* I heard. *It's me. What are you doing? I miss you. Listen, I got tickets to see the Yankees and Mets tonight. You'll love it—it's called the Subway Series. It will be fun. I'll see you tonight.*

I smiled and thought, How lucky am I? This is the love I have always waited for, and now I have it—*wait, what's that?* The machine was still running. Billy hadn't hung up the phone. I listened closely to the message and hear him talking yet on another phone:

Hey, what's up? I'll take a hundred. Where? Don't be giving me any of that crappy shit [laughing]. *I'm just kidding. Okay, sounds good, later.*

I stood there in shock.

Should I have *been* in shock? I had known the issue existed at *some* point—bits and pieces of stories that I'd heard. Maybe I just had a case of "selective hearing." Did I think Billy and drugs just magically *disappeared,* or had I chosen to ignore them?

The next day, I played it back to him. He didn't deny it. I told him he could not stay unless he entered a drug treatment center. He agreed. We found one that would take his insurance, and off he went. I made sure I wrote him a letter every night he was there and included how proud I was of him and how much I loved him.

He was only there for three days.

He's coming out already? I thought.

When I got the call from his brother that he wanted me to pick him up, I was very concerned. Three days was not enough, but on the flip side, I missed him terribly and couldn't wait to see him.

Once again, my desire to be with him overrode any danger signs that might have been flashing—and if I saw them, I rapidly didn't care. I was hoping it wasn't that serious, that maybe he would just stop. Little did I know that Billy was slowly becoming *my* drug. I was in love and needed to be with him, and I wasn't about to give him up.

My instructions were to pick him up in the Mustang at

9:00 a.m. I got up extra early and made sure I looked my best. I jumped in the black muscle car, and off I went. I entered the establishment a little nervous but excited that I could wrap my arms around him again. I heard a lot of clapping going on. Then I saw Billy ambling toward me.

"There she is," he said with a big smile. He was holding his arms wide open, and I fell into them and we hugged as though a year had passed. He started to tell me about his experience. He said the other patients had nick-named him "Travolta," and that, at night, he was so hungry he would sneak down to the kitchen and make himself a peanut-butter-and-jelly sandwich.

We started driving home, his hand on mine, only leaving it to change gears. It was a gorgeous day, the radio was on, and the sun was shining. He glanced over at times, and we would look at each other. I would see the love in his eyes, and I'm sure he saw the love in mine.

I lowered the radio, turned to him, and said, "Billy, I have something to tell you."

Still driving, he glanced at me. I said, "I'm pregnant."

He looked at me and put a huge smile on his face. He grabbed my hand, looking very happy.

"Really!" he said.

We pulled over and held each other. He gave me a soft kiss gently on the lips. Smiling and very excited he said,

"Come on, let's go tell my brother."

14

ROBIN WILLIAMS

I had been living out a life of excitement ever since I joined my agency. I'd been a part of many projects and met the most interesting people. Every job took me to a different place. When I worked on *Law and Order: SVU*, there would always be a celebrity guest—an actor from a past television show or someone current. It was always a nice surprise to find out who would be on set that day.

Traveling into the city was not hard, but with my poor sense of direction I always wanted to hook up with a group of extras and share the ride. One day I got a call from the agency to do *Law and Order: SVU*. Usually it shot in New Jersey, which was very convenient, but this episode required traveling into the city. I was a little tired and not feeling up to it that week, so I thought I would sit it out, which was unusual for me. The night after the job was scheduled, I called a friend I knew, who had gone, to ask about the guest who'd starred on the episode.

"Hi, Eric. How'd it go today? Who was on the show?"

"You're not going to believe it, Don—it was Robin Williams! It was *amazing*. We all had a pillow fight in the park with him until the feathers were flying out. He was the special guest star because it was their two hundredth episode."

"Robin Williams! I can't believe it. . .the one time I didn't go. . . . How was it? Did you get close to him? What was he like?"

"I wasn't that close—there was a big crowd of people there. He was somewhere in the middle. It was a blast, though. Sorry you missed it."

How many opportunities do you get in life to work with Robin Williams? *This* time I was not going to miss out. I knew that every episode ended with a court scene. This meant they had to film one, and soon. I'd been on the show enough times to know the drill: It's usually done last, so I had time. I *have* to call Barbara at the agency, I decided.

"Hi, Barbara. It's Don."

"How are you, sweetheart?"

"Barbara, can you please, please, *please* get me on *Law and Order: SVU* if they call? It's very important. I think Robin Williams might be on as a guest."

"Okay—if they call, I'll give you a ring."

She called later that evening and told me she'd booked me for the next morning.

"Thank you, Barbara, you're the best! Did they tell you who was on?"

"No, they never give out that information."

"Okay, thanks again."

I SHOWED UP EARLY THAT MORNING with my three sets of wardrobe in tow, praying my theory was right. It didn't look any different around the set, as if a big major star was coming. I guess in my mind it was somehow supposed to.

I started to ask around to see if anyone knew he was going to be there that day, but no one seemed to know.

Time went on. We began filling out our paperwork and getting ready for our wardrobe check. I had started to give up hope when I overheard two guys talking. They seemed excited about something. I turned to them and asked if they knew who the guest star was.

They said in sync, with wide grins and that look of excitement in their eyes, *"Robin Williams!"* Bingo...*yes!*

Some people will argue that actors are just ordinary people like you and me, that they too put their pants on one leg at a time.

Actually, they're not—their ability to make you laugh or cry, and reaching you in a way like no other, makes them special. If they take you away from your pain, even if only for a minute, or give you some pleasure in life, it's a priceless gift that makes them far from ordinary.

I could hardly wait for them to call us to go into the mock courtroom, where we would be seated in the gallery. I was lucky enough to get one of the front seats.

Then, there he was.

I saw him right away as we entered the set. He was wearing dark-rimmed glasses for the part, but you knew exactly who he was. Even though he was right in front of me, it was so surreal. All the fantastic movies he'd been in, what a talent. I felt so lucky to be there; I had been given a rare opportunity to watch him work behind the scenes. What a privilege.

We all watched him in awe. Between takes, he was not only joking around with the major players, he paid attention to all of us, too, which made us smile and laugh the whole time. He was so funny.

He singled out one extra on the jury. She looked a lot like Halle Berry. He said something like, "Look Halle Berry's in the house, and does anyone realize that Halle Berry is on the jury?"

It was something along those lines but a whole lot funnier. We all laughed, and it put a big smile on her face. Even though the role he was playing was serious, between takes he continued to entertain us in typical Robin Williams fashion, with those impressions and sounds of anything and everything that came into that brilliant mind of his.

Like Mariska Hargitay, there was another actress on the show who was very down-to-earth. She treated extras with the same amount of courtesy and respect as she did anyone else on the show. Her name is Dianne Neal. She played Casey Novak, the assistant district attorney. I don't know if she'd known Robin Williams before that day or had just met him, but they palled around like they'd known each other for years. They hung out together, playfully joking back and forth. They seemed to really enjoy each other's company. If I remember correctly, she did say she too had been a comedian at one time. You could certainly tell she was also very excited he was there as well.

They say some comedians onstage seem outgoing but are actually very shy offstage. That was the case with Robin

Williams. Sometimes, the person smiling and laughing is in the most pain. I've experienced depression, as I've said. I can always spot someone else who suffers. I can usually tell when I see them alone and they think no one is watching. A certain expression appears on their faces. I know it all too well.

After Mr. Williams was done doing the scene, the director called for a break. I quickly walked out ahead, so I could hang out in the hallway, thinking he might say something to me as he walked by. From the time the director yelled, "cut," Robin Williams was joking and smiling. But when he emerged alone into the dim, wide hallway, his whole demeanor changed. It was as if a light switch had been turned off. I saw the look that I spoke about on his face. I'd read that he didn't like to cheat anyone out of the whole "Robin Williams experience." It must have been hard to feel the need to be "on" all the time, hard at that time performing while going through personal problems—hard at times to be Robin Williams.

The next moment, one of the new extras went right up to him and asked him for an autograph. Mr. Williams was not rude but, in a nice way, said, "Oh, please, not now, maybe later." I guess that kid hadn't got the memo. We were not supposed to ask for autograph or pictures. We are all supposed to be working.

What a tremendous performance Mr. Williams turned in. The whole premise of the show was not to be a sheep. . .a follower. Are you simply going to do something or stay somewhere because someone tells you to? Are doctors always right? Think for yourself. They actually brought a live sheep in for the episode. She was a star in her own right, having performed in the Christmas show they put on every year in New York City. (Of course, I got a picture with her.) The episode was a dramatic role that Mr. Williams mastered. The guest appearance left me wanting more of his character, but don't we always want more of Robin's characters? From what I understand, he had loved to tease Pam Dawber on the set of *Mork and Mindy*. At one point during the taping he began to teasing Mariska Hargitay. She was wearing an all-green outfit. If memory serves, he playfully started singing Irish tunes, with an Irish brogue, doing what he did, joking around. She was a good sport and laughed it off. After a while, she finally said with a smile, "Robin, did you forget to take your medication today?" But it was all in good fun.

Once again, we were called out for a change of wardrobe. Robin was coming down the same corridor with Dianne Neal. The same kid went rushing up to him, asking him again for an autograph.

Diane Neal, all smiles, said, "Oh, you want an autograph? Sure."

Robin signed his autograph and gave it to him. I was, like, all bets are off—I'm getting a picture with him. I walked right up to them.

"Can I get a picture, please?"

I kind of looked at Diane with eagerness in my eyes. I knew she would make it happen.

She said, "Sure."

I'd always planned on telling Robin a joke if I ever spoke to him, one I thought he would appreciate. I turned to him and asked him if he wanted to hear one.

He said, "Okay."

"How do you catch a unique rabbit?"

"How?"

"You neek up on it."

I can't even say how he reacted. I was so nervous, I don't remember. After that, I stood close beside him, and Diane took the picture with my camera. He said something sweet after that, like, "Thank you, dear." I think he smiled; I don't know if he even heard my joke. I was too starstruck.

GEORGE CARLIN WROTE, "Just because the monkey is off your back doesn't mean the circus has left town." I believe he was commenting on the struggles of drug addiction. I think the statement could apply as well to depression: Just because you have a stretch of time feeling good, you know the darkness is always there and can come over you at any time, without warning. Nobody will ever know the pain of depression and anxiety unless they have been through it. Seeing a loved one go through it is no picnic either.

Jim Carrey has said, "I think everybody should get rich and famous and do everything they ever dreamed of, so they can see that it's not the answer."

This I already knew even without having those things. You can't buy happiness, especially if you suffer from depression—it's not for sale. Pray to God, your higher power, or whatever you believe to help you. To come into money could, in fact, be the worst thing for a depressed person or drug addict. You wouldn't have to work; you'd have no responsibilities, eventually no reason to get out of bed. And for a drug addict, that money would be as good as gone—if you lived to see the end of it.

Everyone on that set, in that mock court room that day, was treated to something really fine. I cherish the memory of a truly gifted actor and unique spirit. He will live on in our hearts and minds through his great performances.

I must tell you: I was looking for a place to work on this chapter. In Livingston, New Jersey, I came across a New York Bagel shop that I used to pass all the time but never entered. I decided for some reason to pull over and go in that day. As I was writing, while I sipped my coffee, I thought, *I wonder how Robin Williams would feel about me writing about him.*

I started to feel sad about what he went through. At that moment, I happened to look up and couldn't believe my eyes. At the next table—right in front me—I thought I was seeing things. It was Robin Williams. I did a double take, because it was just too much to digest.

I said, "Sir, excuse me—do you know you look exactly like Robin Williams?"

He smiled and said, "Yes, I get that all the time."

I held up my journal. "I'm doing a book, and I'm writing about him right now."

He smiled again. The people next to us, who had overheard the conversation, couldn't get over how much this man resembled him either. I asked him if I could take a picture of him. He was more than happy to oblige.

I don't know, what do *you* think? You already know what I do.

15

CLOUD NINE

AFTER LEAVING BILLY'S BROTHER TONY'S, we stopped at his mom's to tell her the good news. She seemed happy but a little weary. Roe and I had grown close over the years because of my involvement with Noah's kids. She'd told me once that she wanted me with one of her sons, but I think she knew there were a lot of unresolved issues in Billy's life. He was not yet divorced and had just been released from a treatment center. Regardless, as long as Billy was happy, at that point, she was.

I couldn't believe I was a having a baby, his baby, *our* baby. I was so in love with him and regularly asking myself, *Can this really be happening to me?* To finally find him again, and to be together and have a family—in a perfect world, all of it would be *wonderful*. I guess my head was in the clouds as much as his. I ignored all the warning signs and remained in some fairytale, thinking everything was going to end Happily Ever After.

Billy left for work the next morning. I was still on cloud nine, planning to tell my mother the news that day, when the doorbell rang. I opened the door to find a dozen red roses sitting there in a beautiful vase. The card that came with them read, *Now you're really more than a woman to me, Love, Billy.* (That was our song, recorded by the Bee Gees.)

Everything was perfect. I was babysitting for a friend and had grown very attached to her child. The family was from another state, so they mainly relied on me to help them out while they worked. I'd never been pregnant, so I was sure something could be worked out, that I could still be there for them up until I was close to giving birth. Their mom could fly in for my maternity leave until I got back; then my mom could take over. I had it all worked out.

As the days went on, Billy often told me he was going to the firehouse. Every time he came back, I knew that he had done something else, though, and I came to the conclusion that he was using again. In recovery, you're advised to attend regular meetings, find a sponsor, and stay away from stressful situations—but the situation he was in was anything but.

We had made plans to have a dinner with my mother and father. It was the first time he'd really met them. He got along great with my father. My mother loved the way he did his hair. It reminded her of the fifties. It looked the way James Dean and Elvis had done theirs. My father and Billy talked about everything. They both came from humble backgrounds, had worked hard, and climbed up the ladder to a better life. It was nice to finally show my parents what I loved about him, especially my mother.

Billy had consulted his lawyer about my pregnancy. She was not a happy camper and put pressure on him to move out of my apartment. She explained to him that it would look very bad that he was accusing his wife of cheating while he was living with his girlfriend—and had a baby on the way.

When he told me he was going to move out, I became very upset. I felt vulnerable. I was afraid things were going to change. He told me he would get an apartment close to me, and that his wife could not find out about the pregnancy. The lawyer told him if his wife did find out, it would make the situation worse, and that Billy could possibly lose everything in court.

He couldn't handle the situation emotionally. Reality started to set in—having a baby in the middle of everything, afraid his kids would not love him anymore, and trying to be there for me.

I too was slipping into a very bad place. I tried to hide it by staying at my mother's house. I would call him and make an excuse about why I had to. I had a hard time working. I *had* to get back on my anti-depression med. I could feel myself falling into that deep, horrific hole again. I was afraid I was going to get to the point where I couldn't function. What was I going to do? *I can't take medicine*, I told myself. *I don't want to do anything to hurt our baby. Is any medicine safe? Where do I go? Whom do I ask?*

I had taken a couple of days off to try to pull myself together. My mom went with me to the doctor. I needed to find a treatment that was safe for the baby *and* could help me function again.

He put me on a medication that made me feel like I was going to jump out of my skin, but he said it was the safest one you could take during pregnancy.

On the way back from the doctor's office, I stopped by my apartment. I saw Billy's big plumbing truck parked outside, and one of his employees loading all his things. I couldn't believe that he was leaving like that. He hadn't even told me.

I just broke down to my mother. I started to cry and told her that I wasn't going to be able to handle it. I went back to her house. I was certain he was going to leave me.

I got a message that night to tell me that he'd gotten his stuff while I was at work. He'd thought it would be better that I was not there.

I was so upset I found it hard to call him. I hadn't even known he'd already gotten an apartment. I waited for the next morning.

"Hi, Billy, it's me. Why did you just leave like that? You didn't even tell me you found an apartment."

"I knew how upset you would be," he said, "so I didn't want to tell you."

"So you just leave while I'm at *work?*"

"It's close to your mom's house like you wanted, so when you stay there, we'll be close. I still left some things at the apartment. . . . I have to do something for work. I'll call you tonight."

He used to call me three times a day, and he'd given me my own special phone that was actually a walkie-talkie-like thing on which we could contact each other at a moment's notice. Things had already changed. This was not happening.

Billy did call me that night, but he didn't invite me over. I asked him what he was doing. He said he was going to get together with some friends. I guess, since he was not under my roof anymore and I wasn't helping him out, all bets were off. I was beside myself. I said, "Okay," and he said he would call me the next day.

He never did.

I couldn't concern myself with him, however, because I was in trouble and I knew it. I was losing control and slipping deeper into the anxiety-ridden place I'd barely gotten out of the last time. I had to do something. I couldn't go back there. I had to go to work. I couldn't lose my job.

My mother and father knew I was in bad shape and called Dana; she was a nurse and was always there for us in any kind of crisis. She found another doctor we could go to right away.

I had asked him about the medication I had been on in the past. He told me he thought it would be okay to take it during pregnancy. It didn't work as quickly or as well as it had before (I assumed my body chemistry maybe was different because I was pregnant), but it was better than the stuff the other doctor had prescribed.

I stayed at my place, hoping to hear from Billy. Maybe he needed some time. Now that he had no one to come home to, he had free reign to do whatever he wanted...and that included getting into trouble.

A couple of nights later, I was lying on the couch in my apartment when the phone rang. It was Billy.

"How can you *do* this to me?" he exclaimed frantically.

"What am I going to *do* now?"

"...What are you *talking* about, Billy?"

"You *trapped me!* Now my kids are going to hate me, and when my soon-to-be ex finds out, she's going to take me for *everything!* My lawyer made that very clear."

He sounded drunk. I couldn't believe what he was saying. He told me to pack up the rest of his things, that he wanted them. I couldn't speak. I hung up the phone and went to my mother's a total mess.

I couldn't work anymore and knew it—especially taking care of kids. How was I going to tell my boss? They had just had another baby, and I didn't want to jeopardize their safety. I had to call. How was I going to pay my bills? I was going to lose everything.

I told her the truth, that I was in bad shape. She asked me when I could come back. I told her I didn't know. To this day, I am so grateful for her and her husband for being as understanding as they were. I put them in such a bad spot.

I stayed at my mother's. I went upstairs into one of my brothers' old empty rooms. With the light off, I lay on the bed in a fetal position. Although the situation was inherently very painful, being in that state made it feel like death. I had lost the little girl I watched whom I loved so much; the guy I thought loved me had betrayed me in the worst way, and all my bills were going to pile up. The worst thing of all was that I lost my peace of mind. I was in that horrible place again, with these losses almost too much to bear. I knew that, if I fell asleep, I would have to wake up—mornings are the worst. Anyone who suffers from depression can attest to that.

16

BLACK HOLE

SINCE THE MEDICATION I had once been on was not working this time, as predicted, my mornings were indeed the worst. I spent the days at my parents' house and went back to my apartment at night. I listened to a meditation CD with my earphones on, hoping it would help me feel better. At times I closed my eyes and imagined myself and my unborn child holding hands and dancing in a circle. I guess in some strange way I was calling on my baby to comfort me. I had to focus on something positive. I kept that image in my mind.

Oh, God, I prayed, *please don't let me slip into that horrid black hole that I know only too well.* Why did I go off my medication? I'm so stupid, I thought. I don't think this time I can survive. But I have to, I have my baby inside me. But I won't take any more medication than I have to, no matter how bad I feel. I didn't want to go to sleep. No one who hasn't experienced depression and anxiety can fully conceive how horrid it can be. No one who hasn't experienced depression and anxiety can fully conceive how horrid it can be. I meant to say that twice.

I heard Billy wasn't doing well either. I think the reality of his situation started to sink in, and it was a lot to deal with all at once. The things he was doing to numb his pain were not helping his state of mind; they were only making it worse.

You can't be in a marriage for almost twenty years, have it end, and not be affected. It doesn't matter who ended it, why, or what the reasons were—there still was a love there, and there were children. Whether for the best or not in the long run, it remained a tremendous loss. It takes a long time to recover from a broken relationship, time Billy didn't take. There is no way around grief. Alcohol and other stimulants will only prolong the process. You have to go straight through it head on and feel the pain, or you will never heal.

I was sitting alone in my apartment. My feelings of anxiety were better at night for some reason, so I decided to give Gina a call. She told me that she had just been on the phone with Billy. He was driving around town and had passed her house. I hung up with her and, without thinking, dialed his number. He picked up and sounded happy to hear from me. I could tell he was drinking. "Don! Hi...hi," he said in a shaky voice. "I'm sorry...I'm sorry. Can I come over...*please?*"

I couldn't believe it, but I said he could. I waited outside, not truly thinking about what I was doing or why. Then, out of the darkness, he came up the stairs, came toward me, fell into my arms, and started crying hysterically. He was very drunk and very upset.

I embraced him just as intensely as he was holding me. I loved him so much, but we were both what you might call a "hot mess." If we were ever going to reconnect in our life, at this point, was definitely the wrong time.

We went into the bedroom and made love. I guess I could have had him with me after that for a month or two, maybe six, but the truth was I couldn't function. I was in such bad shape that, if he hurt me again, it would do me in. The mornings I think were bad for him as well; I glanced in the living room and saw him smoking a cigarette with a face filled with anxiety. I went back to bed and pretended to be asleep.

Late that morning he called me and asked me if everything was alright. I was feeling horrible. I started to cry and barked, "*No,* everything's *not alright.* I can't *work.* I'm losing *everything!*"

Why did he have to treat me that way and get me to this point? I thought. We both hung up the phone. I had to stay away from him. He had hurt me so badly the first time, I couldn't risk it—it would surely put me over the edge. I had to concentrate on not slipping into the point of no return, avoiding that dreadful darkness that was all too familiar.

We were both supposed to go to my childhood friend's wedding out of state. We had seen each other almost every day while growing up. I was in the wedding party. I tried to go, but each day my anxiety was taking me over more and more. When my mother took me to shop for the shoes for the bridesmaid's dress, it took everything I had to go with her. I often had trouble breathing, which was part of the anxiety. In the store, I ran into some of Billy's friends. Shortly after, I received a phone call from him. He asked me to come over to his apartment and watch a movie. I really wanted to, but I couldn't. I couldn't even exist in my own skin, let alone be around him.

I had Dana break the news to my friend that I couldn't be in her wedding. I just couldn't tell her. Dana went in my place. She always came to my rescue. I made sure to give my friend an envelope, but I knew it wouldn't make up for not being there. I'd really hurt her, which only added to my guilt and anxiety.

Karen has always told me, "Look for the warning signs. You see them, get out of there." I had looked past them, somehow rationalized them. Billy would say, "Aren't you pregnant yet?" He would refer to me with his last name, as if we were going to be married someday. I thought my prince had arrived, that we found each other again after all those years and were going to live happily ever after.

Who's to blame? I wondered.

17

STARSTRUCK

GOING BACK, I WAS ENJOYING my little girl immensely. My mother was helping me 24/7. I had the best of both worlds, being a mom and at the same time participating in a world one could only fantasize about. I didn't have time to be depressed—I was either enjoying precious moments taking care of my child, or I was on a set, involved in an exciting movie or TV show. As I said earlier, every set was a different adventure.

There was talk *The Sopranos* was going to pack it in soon. I only hoped that I would have the opportunity to be a part of one of the last seasons. I'd come too far to give up hope. I had faith that John would try to fill his "ninety-nine percent" promise. After all, they *were* great odds.

The phone calls for work continued. There were times when the jobs were not so glamorous, but they were few and far between. Being an "extra or background" is sometimes not easy. The hours can be long, and there's a lot of waiting around. On the flip side, you can shoot one scene, which can require you to run a good distance, climb a flight of stairs, and go through a revolving door. If they don't get the shot right away, you may have to repeat these five or six times. One of my jobs was particularly tiring—a movie called *Fighting*. We wound up working all night. People were sleeping standing up as they waited on line to sign themselves out in the wee hours. Shooting one of the scenes that day, I happened to see the lead actor in the movie. Young and very attractive, he was standing right next to me. I remember thinking he was a newcomer and disappointed that there was no major star there.

That cute actor turned out to be Channing Tatum. It was one of his earliest films.

John Travolta had been one of my big favorites growing up. He is from Englewood, New Jersey, close to where I was born and raised. I heard a rumor about a movie that he was going to star in, and that they were looking for extras. I communicated routinely with my friends in the agency to see where they were going and what sets they were going to be on. I called Eric one day to see what he was up to. If there was something going on, he was the one that would know about it.

"Oh, hi," he said. "How have you been? I haven't seen you in a couple of weeks."

"I know, it's been crazy. Have you been on any jobs?"

"Actually, John called me today—I'm going on one tomorrow. It's at the airport. John Travolta's supposed to be in it."

"Really? I'm going to call him. I *love* John Travolta.

Maybe John can see if there's a spot for me. I hope so! Thanks Eric, I'll talk to you soon."

I immediately dialed the familiar number. "Hi, John, it's Don. Eric's going to the airport tomorrow to be in that movie with John Travolta."

"I know, I sent him."

"I *love* John Travolta. Do you think I can go, too? Are there anymore spots left?

"None as of now. I can call you if one opens. . .you know what? Just go down there. There's always one person I book that doesn't show up. It's worth a shot if it really means that much to you."

"It does. Thanks, John!"

John Travolta now, are you kidding me? I can't believe it. When I was in grade school, a classmate told me that her father and he were really good friends, and that John Travolta had been at the hospital when she was born. True or not, she told me he was possibly coming to her house for Christmas dinner that year. We exchanged numbers, and she said maybe I could talk to him. I waited in my room, by my phone, but no call came. I decided to call her, but an answering machine picked up. Wow, I thought, she must be rich—she has an *answering machine.*

John Travolta's character in *Saturday Night Fever* reminded me of Billy when he was young. I must have seen *Grease* a million times. I dressed up as the "cool" Sandy for Halloween when I was in seventh grade. I wore tight leather pants, a curly blonde wig, and a leather jacket. Don't ask me how I went around from house to house trick or treating in my mom's old '50s red spike heels, but I did.

On the day of the job, I was beyond excited. The wardrobe instruction was to wear bright colors and busy patterns, something upbeat. I wore a long rain jacket I had bought on a trip to Vegas. It had a black-and-white zebra pattern. I showed up and took the place of a no-show.

But then I discovered it wasn't John Travolta in the movie, it was Kevin Bacon. He was dressed in a military outfit. The movie was *Taking Chance*. I was just as excited, but a little disappointed, too.

We were instructed to sit in the airport waiting area. At one point I sat almost directly across from him. I wanted to go over and tell him how my mother loved his wife's TV show, which was running then. I eventually looked his way. I tried not to stare, but I guess I might have. His eyebrows began going up and down very fast. . .I don't know if that was meant for me or not. I looked behind me, and there was nobody there; I guess I'll never know. I imagine people staring at you all the time can get annoying.

The bus for the extras was too full, so my friend and I, along with some other people, had to go on Kevin Bacon's bus. Yes, I rode on a bus with Kevin Bacon. That may not be a thrill for some, but it was for me. This movie turned out to be a must-see; it was based on a book written by the man Kevin Bacon was playing. As he has done in all of his films, Mr. Bacon's great acting brought the character to life. I'm sure he made everyone involved proud.

After the bus ride, my cell phone rang. It was John, calling to see if I had made it through and filled in for somebody. "Hey, Don, did everything work out? Did you get in okay?"

"Yes, I did, John, but you said John Travolta was going to be here. He's not...it's Kevin Bacon."

"Oh, sorry, Don," he said and added sarcastically, "Isn't Kevin Bacon good enough for you?"

"Yes, of course. Thank you! This is great!"

"Okay. Just try to get a picture—it'll be good for the agency."

"Okay, I will."

I didn't. I asked Mr. Bacon's assistant instead of him while they were both walking in the lunch area. I should have asked him instead. It was, anyhow, another day I won't soon forget.

Photo Gallery

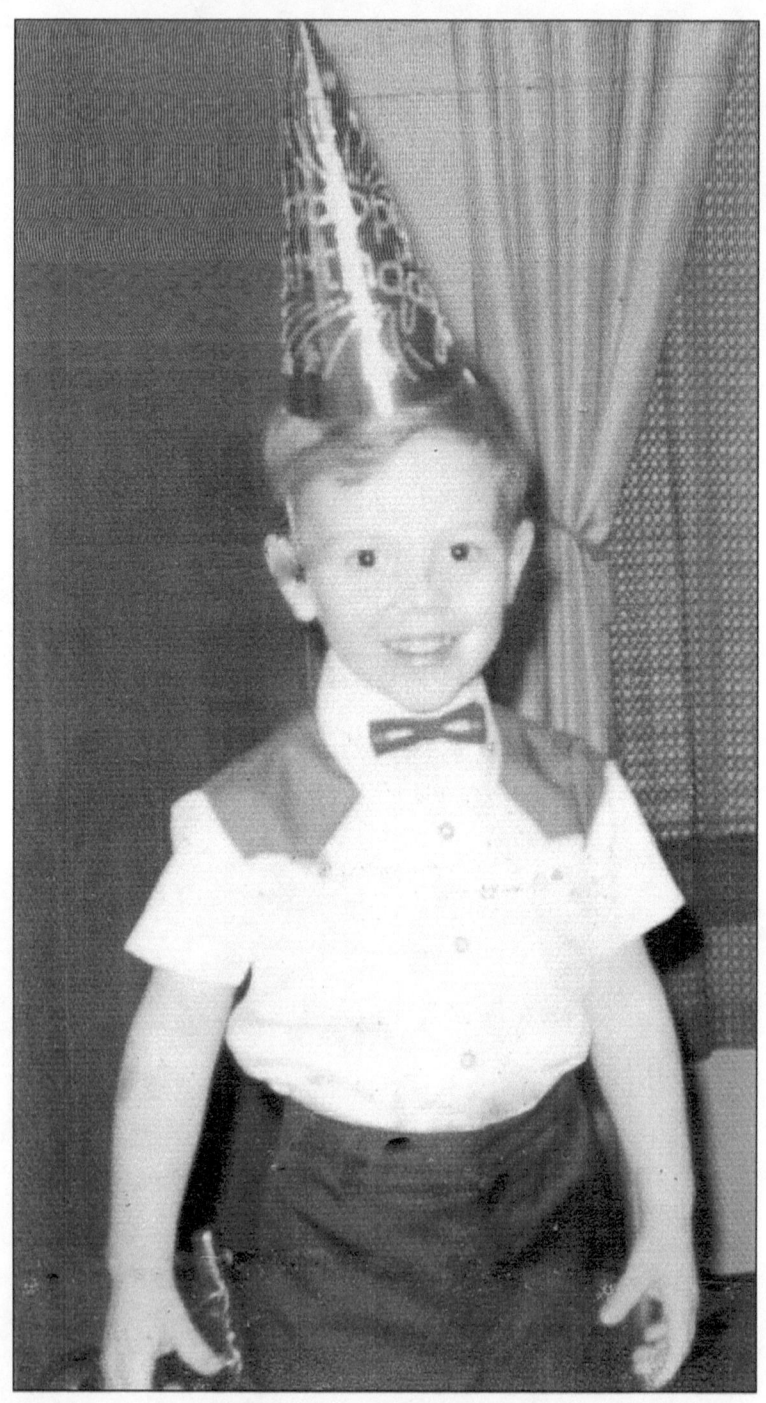
My youngest brother, who passed away from melanoma at 39

January 2006—"I Am Legend." Hundreds of movie extras gather by the Brooklyn Bridge, waiting for their cue from the director.

January 2006—my acting partner Toni Ann (right) and me, warming up in the tent while filming "I Am Legend" with Will Smith

Denis Leary and me "Rescue Me" on location, the Bears and Eagles Riverfront Stadium in Newark, New Jersey

One of the stars and me—"Law and Order SUV"s 200th episode celebration, starring Robin Williams

My precious daughter, 2007, on one of the rides "down the shore" in New Jersey

March 2007—one of the pictures I took posing as a reporter.

18

EUPHORIA

IF YOU MAKE THE CONSCIOUS DECISION to do drugs, you will most certainly end up like someone who chooses to be in the Mafia. In *The Sopranos*, Christopher went that route at one point in his life. Tony even gave him a pass, though he should have been whacked. Ultimately, he ended up having to kill him anyway. You can't blame Tony; he tried to help him, although it was a tremendous risk. After Tony and Christopher had the car accident, lying injured on the ground, Christopher told Tony that he would test positive. He had no choice. Can you say Witness Protection Program?

The pull of drugs is so strong. Case in point: The fear of Tony Soprano's wrath didn't scare Christopher. The drug was stronger than the fear. If you don't stop using drugs, one of two things *are* going to happen. You'll wind up dead or in jail.

But not *initially*.

Crack cocaine will give you a feeling of pleasure that one could never imagine. One long inhale on that round glass pipe feels like euphoria—not to mention your sex drive, will go through the roof. The pleasure of sex is phenomenal. You'll literally want to screw each other in every way possible, fast, long, and hard while taking hits and deeply inhaling the smoke of this forbidden fruit.

"Hold it is as long as possible," he says as his hard body is thrusting in and out, deep into yours.

A porno playing, this drug in your system while being taken from behind, is enough to make you want to scream at the top of your lungs while your body is riddled with pleasure. It only lasts about two and half minutes, though, and then you want more. Nobody has to try to sell you this drug after the first try—it sells itself.

A compulsive liar, that's what you are now. No one is important, only the drug. When you're done, and there is no more, coming down in horrific, the depression unbearable. The next day, you think of all the money you owe the dealers—wait a minute, it *is* the next day, the sun is up. This fact only adds to your misery. You swear you will never do it again. You go home, lie down, and pray the feeling of death will pass.

In your mind, you're saying over and over to yourself, "I'll never do this again, I'll never do this again."

You sleep for hours. When you wake up, it's late afternoon and you're feeling better. You go about your day but don't realize that what you do with your time, and whom you agree to see, are all part of a subconscious plan, the addictions way of eventually getting more. The drug has a mind of its own. You start to think of ways to not only pay off your loan but get your hands on more money. You've become a master manipulator, a compulsive liar, a horrible friend, daughter, sister. You find yourself seeking it again—borrowing, taking cash advances, using gift cards and savings, selling jewelry, making sordid exchanges. You spend hundreds (thousands) of dollars digging yourself in a tremendous financial hole. Soon, all your money is gone.

And this is just a sugar-coated version of the start of your downward spiral. If you can't stop, your behavior can reach a more pathetic level of "rock bottom" along with your dignity and self-worth, all in exchange for chasing the initial two-and-a-half-minute high...give or take.

They call a crack pipe "the devil's dick." You feel all this pleasure when you suck on it. It takes you and your body to great places. You're having fun, but there will be—not *maybe*, there *will be* a price. It's going to stop being fun. As you keep using the drug, in time the paranoia will set in. You're going to think you hear the police coming to break down your motel door when, actually, there's nobody there...or *is* there? You keep thinking at that moment they might be staking out the place. You start peeking out from behind the curtains to see. You try to have sex but can't enjoy it because your state of mind had changed into pretty much that of a paranoid idiot. You hear footsteps again—here they come. You dive out of bed and sit with your back pushed tightly against the door with all your weight, as if that's going to stop them. Spray the room, spray the room, the smell, you loudly whisper in a state of jumpy paranoia. You start frantically spraying air freshener.

"I have to get out of here. I'm trapped! I'm going to *jail!*"

You run out and find someplace to get more liquor to calm you down. You come back; there's none left; you want more. You look in the corner and find that you dropped a gigantic rock on the floor. The excitement you feel comes close to just finding a million dollars. You share and enjoy it immensely. Maybe there is another one. You then find yourself crawling pitifully on your hands and knees across a germ-filled motel carpet, looking for another crumb to put in your glass pipe. The feeling can't end. You want *more*.

You call your dealers to see which one answers. You have no money. They'll give you credit, but you have to pay double for the same quantity, and they want the money the next day. You agree, swearing you'll have it, though you know you won't.

You do these things three or four times. They've just earned a hundred percent interest. You rush back to the motel. You can't wait. . . .

And then it's done already. *I want more.* There is none. The sun is up.

You will start to eventually resemble a homeless person. You can't stop. It has a mind of its own. You never want the feeling to end, even *with* the paranoia. You're chasing your high. The person you once were to people will be gone. They know something is wrong, but they can't put their finger on it. You put on a façade.

And this is nothing compared to how low people will go and what they will do for drugs.

Congratulations. . .you just sold your soul.

19

FIVE LITTLE WORDS

THERE'S A SAYING THAT I HEARD around the recovery forum that goes, "I'll get you high before you get me straight." That, for me, means you have to be careful trying to get somebody you love sober because, in certain situations, you could find yourself in a vulnerable state.

They also say, "If you can't beat them, join them." One of the five steps to recovery advises not to let yourself get "too lonely."

I wasn't doing drugs, but I had an addiction—to Billy. Healthy people would have steered clear of the whole situation. They would not have tried to return to a person who had treated them so poorly under any circumstances. But I was not a healthy person, nor was he, at the time.

This was my pattern: Instead of valuing myself, as Karen would put it, and seeing my involvement with him for what it was, a no-win situation, I marched ahead. Having been put down and rejected so much in my early life, I see now, what happened between us had opened old, painful wounds of rejection and loneliness.

A couple of years nonetheless went by; little by little, the smoke of my anger started to clear toward Billy. I had the most beautiful daughter and was so grateful for her, but I found myself feeling an emptiness inside that I knew only too well. I had gone from someone loving me completely, doing every possible thing for me, to being a single mother. Watching my daughter on rides down the shore was hard for me for some reason, too. I would see all the couples holding hands, laughing, and waving at their kids, and I was always standing alone.

Billy was by then on his second relationship, and I still couldn't believe how things could have gone so wrong. How could they not, given the circumstances?—*that's* really what I should have asked myself.

One night, a desperate urge to see him came over me in a wave. I couldn't wait. Everything had come to a head; I had to see him, I felt desperate. I couldn't not be with him for another second.

"Hi, Billy, it's me. What are you doing?"

"Hey, what's up? I'm on my way home. I want to get an early start, so I don't hit traffic."

"I have to see you for a minute. I have to talk to you. It's important."

". . .Okay, meet me at The Crest on Route 46. I can't stay long, though. I have to get home.

"Okay, I'm leaving now. See you there."

It was a rainy night; I couldn't believe he'd agreed to

meet me. His current girlfriend did not want him anywhere near me. If she found out, he would be in a lot of trouble, especially now that she knew we were on good terms.

Pulling into the parking lot, I could feel my heart racing. In my mind, there was no way I was leaving there without him. I needed him to kiss me. I needed to feel him again. I had let myself get too lonely. All sense had gone out the window, and I needed a fix. I knew for a fact that Billy was still using, and I knew one thing that might lure him to stay.

I walked in and saw him sitting at the bar. He gave me a kiss on the cheek. He was drinking a beer and had already ordered me one. I could tell he wanted our meeting to be short and sweet. We began talking, sitting close to one another at the bar. I ordered a shot for both of us, mainly so I could feel more relaxed. Somehow my hand wound up on top of his.

"So what was so important that you couldn't tell me over the phone?" he asked.

Having the beer and shot down, I was brutally honest. Still holding his hand, I looked up at him and said, "I really miss you."

"I miss you, too. I think about us a lot, but I'm living with someone now, and she's very jealous. She called three times already."

The fact that he had moved on so easily was heartbreaking. The fact that his girlfriend was waiting for him didn't faze me, though. I had one mission, and I was going to accomplish it at any cost. I had no idea what it would cost. Then I spoke these five little words:

"Do you have any coke?"

"...Why do you ask that?

"Because I want to do some with you."

"No, you don't, you're just saying that."

"Really, I do, I'm not kidding. Come on...I know you have some," I said, smiling, as I leaned into him.

"...Do you want to go to a hotel room?"

"Yes, I do."

He instantly said, "Come on, let's get out of here."

20

BONNIE AND CLYDE

I T'S ALWAYS THE WAY—some of the things that make you feel good in life can really be bad for you in the long run. Figures that a drug that takes you to such great heights, that makes you feel like you're on top of the world, will eventually kill you. As I have already said, it doesn't happen right away. It takes your looks, your body, and all your money...and then it kills you.

Billy and I weren't thinking about anything like that on that warm sunny afternoon. We pulled into one of our favorite motels, started smoking our forbidden pipe, and did things that I think would make even Christian Grey blush.

Eventually, we ran out of money, which is always the worst feeling. Leaving the motel, we tried to figure out how we could get more funds. We were driving down the highway, when a car just slowly came out of his lane and drifted into the side of us—hitting our van, *Wham!* with the side of his car and nearly knocked us into the divider. Luckily,

Billy was driving, because he managed to swerve to keep us from crashing. Both cars spun around, but luckily no one was hurt.

We all got out. The guy's little grey sports car seemed to be in good condition, but it was facing in the other direction. He was very good-looking—blonde hair, blue eyes—but clearly very shook up. As he nervously crept towards us, he kept repeating how sorry he was, and that he had no idea what had happened. He didn't know how he happened to end up in our lane.

My van was damaged, but it was very old, and I had planned on selling it to the junkyard that week, so I wasn't too upset. Billy knew that too but saw an opportunity. He asked the guy if he had any cash on him to pay for the damages. The guy reached in his pocket, pulled out his wallet, opened it, and we saw a thick wad of hundred-dollar bills. Billy's eyes literally lit up like two Roman candles.

"How's four hundred?" he said as he slid them out one by one.

"Come on, man...look at the side of her van. That's a lot of damage. You almost killed us. We are going to need more than that."

"Sure, no problem, you're right, you're right. How much do you think will cover it?"

In the distance, I thought I heard sirens coming, and I thought Billy might have a pipe on him. I started to panic and began tapping him nervously on the shoulder.

"Let's go," I whispered, "come on! Before the police come."

"Just give me another minute—I can get more from this

guy. Did you see how many hundreds he had in there?"

"Come on! Let's *go!*"

I eventually had to literally pull him to the car. My heart was racing, but we managed to flee the scene seven hundred dollars richer.

"Woo-hoo! Oh, *yeah!* Why did you pull me out of there? I could have gotten more. Did you see those hundreds?"

"My nerves are shot, Billy. You're crazy!"

We both felt like we'd hit the lottery. It was a definite adrenaline rush. It could not have come at a better time. We quickly made a phone call and checked into our motel.

We didn't feel badly about how we'd gotten the money, either. In the world of drugs, you have no conscience.

It's just about one thing.

SPEAKING OF ADRENALIN RUSHES, another one of my favorite *Sopranos* episodes is when Tony escapes Junior's hit men. That scene was amazing and brilliantly shot.

On a windy day, Tony casually stops and gets a newspaper and bottle of orange juice from a street vendor. In the reflection of his car door window, Tony sees a guy coming towards him with a gun. He has a split-second to react. The guy shoots at him, misses, but explodes the bottle of orange juice he has in his hand. He quickly gets in the car, dodging another bullet. The guy approaches the driver's side and Tony quickly grabs the barrel of the gun and puts him in a choke hold. It certainly got Tony's adrenaline pumping. "Dead now, mother fucker," a second guy says as he approaches the other side of the car.

He shoots, missing Tony, and hits is partner instead. Tony lets him go and the guy drops to the ground. He reaches over grabs the barrel of the shooter's gun, puts the car in drive, and steps on the gas until he falls to the ground. He looks back to see him rolling behind his speeding car. Tony laughs loudly and smiles in victory until he looks ahead and smashes into a parked car at full speed. Airbag out, Tony is draped over the steering wheel, unconscious.

In a strange twist, after the incident, Tony felt alive again and cured of his depression. Maybe fighting off two guys with guns and basically kicking their ass might be an alternative to shock therapy one day, but I highly doubt it. Still taking medication, I do not think any antidepressant could mask the pain after Tony later discovers *who* really is behind his attempted hit.

21

PARANOIA

I ALWAYS LOOKED FORWARD to our meetings. When I wasn't with him, I missed him. Although Billy was with someone else, I still met him for a night of partying and pleasure, just to get my fix. He would then return to his girlfriend, which was about the worst thing I could do for my self-esteem.

As time went on, my feelings on the drug took a turn. The fear of getting caught started to work on me, especially after Billy told me that the cops had come bursting through the door one night when he was with a girl the year before.

He should not have told me that. After that bit of information, that was it for me. We started off by having such a good time; then I'd think I heard people coming, run to the door, and lean my back against it. I pushed as hard as I could, thinking that, any minute, the police were going to knock it down.

Then I needed a drink to calm down.

Billy and I would be in the middle of the greatest sex—he taking me from behind with slow deep thrusts while we both watched a porno flick. Then he'd slow down while loading the pipe.

"Don't move, stay exactly like that. I loaded the pipe for you with a nice big one. Take a deep breath and hold it in for as long as you can."

As I started taking the hit, I felt him go hard as a rock inside me.

Then he went really fast in and out, like a rabbit. I felt like screaming with pleasure. I was soaking wet. It was *so* good—but soon enough the good feeling disappeared and the paranoia started to set in, and I began to imagine that people might be coming. I pictured them walking down the hall, getting ready to burst in at any time. I'd get up in a panic, in the middle of sex, and run to the door and lean my back against it as hard as I could.

"What are you doing?" he whispered. "Stop! . . . You look *ridiculous*. Nobody's coming. Come here, take another hit. I have a nice big one for you."

We'd start again, but after about forty-five seconds of that amazing feeling, I'd imagine yet again that people were coming, and it would start all over again.

Billy got frustrated because it was happening every time we were together. It got to where I would quickly gather my things and leave him in the hotel room, stranded, with no car.

Sometimes I started spraying air freshener like a mad woman every time Billy took a puff, thinking someone would smell it. Peeking out the window every ten minutes was probably not a good idea either, but that didn't stop me. I kept trying to get over my behavior but, in the end, always ran out the door or leaned up against it.

"Don't go to that door, Don. Don't *do* it! Don, if I give you this hit and we start to make love and you run to that door, I'm going to be pissed."

"I won't, I won't, just give me a big one."

"Take off your clothes first"

I did, and so did he, and I would go right down on him, putting him in my mouth, tasting him, loving it as he moaned—I loved it when he moaned. We both took a hit, he got on top of me, and, *wow*, it was so *good*.

Then the fear again. I'd had a couple of drinks before, but it didn't help. I had to get more liquor. I ran out and went to a diner to have a couple of drinks and take the edge off. Not thinking, I went back to our motel room and banged on the door really hard. He finally opened the door and let me in. As he shut the door he began to gag.

"Why did you *do* that? *Bang* like that? I thought you were the cops! I swallowed the whole thing." He kept gagging.

I started to cry. "Why did you do *that* for? You *knew* I was coming back.

"*Because* you were banging on the *door*. . . . I thought it was the *cops*. I swallowed it! The *whole thing!*" He was brought to tears. "I'm sorry, I'm sorry, I wasn't thinking."

It was the wee hours of the morning, and we could not get in touch with anyone to get more. Desperate as we were, Billy took us down to the worst part of Newark to see if he could score. We drove into this big, dark square apartment complex.

Out of nowhere a large group of guys appeared and

walked toward the car. Billy got out, and they surrounded him with the drugs in their hands, talking fast and over one another, desperate to be picked for the three-hundred-dollar purchase.

Billy settled on the guy who gave him the best deal. He even gave Billy his number in case we wanted more. We quickly drove back to the motel excited about our find.

"Now, let's relax and have a nice time, Don, no running to the door."

Billy would always put on the porno channel and often asked me to call the desk so they could change it to a better one. I found it very embarrassing, but I did it regardless. Billy loaded a pipe for me and one for himself. We lit them at the same time and took a deep breath in. In the next second, we both began to choke uncontrollably, and a toxic smell filled the room.

"What the fuck *is* this shit?" Billie said, really pissed. He took another piece, put it in a clean pipe, and lit it up. The same odor started to fill the room; he continued to smoke it I guess he was hoping it was going to magically turn into something else. He started gagging and threw down the pipe.

"Billy, it's cement. They ripped us *off!*"

"Where's that guy's fuckin' number? He better take this shit back and give me what I *paid* for!"

Billy called the number, and the guy actually picked up.

"You ripped us off, *asshole*. I'm coming down there, and you better have my fucking money."

We both got in the car and headed down there. Billy was really pissed.

"Billy," I said, "let's just go back. We are going to get *killed* down here."

He ignored my suggestion and entered the dark complex and parked in the middle. There was nobody there. He got out of the car and called the guy on his cell; he didn't pick up.

"Where the fuck *are* you?" Billy shouted several times.

"Billy, get in the car! My nerves are shot. He's not going to come out."

Not a good night for a couple of druggies.

In reality, which we were far from, the stuff could have been rat poisoning and we could have been stabbed or shot that night. It served us right for being so stupid. Speaking of getting ripped off, it brings me to one of my other favorite characters and scenes from the Soprano's.

Furio Giunta (played brilliantly by Federico Castelluccio) was an Italian mobster from Italy. He came to America and started working for Tony Soprano to set up an international car theft operation. Witnessing his loyal and ruthless nature to protect his former boss in Italy, Tony wanted him as his bodyguard and debt collector as well.

Arthur ("Artie") Bucco (played beautifully by John Ventimiglia), who is Tony's best friend, lent fifty thousand dollars at a high interest rate to his restaurant hostess's French brother, Jean-Phillippe. He borrowed the money from Tony. The guy wound up ripping him off and beat him up as well. Humiliated, Artie overdosed on alcohol and pills. Tony was distraught that his friend had tried to take his own life, upset that Artie would do such a thing, and worked something out with the money owed.

In the next scene, Jean-Phillippe opens his door, and standing there is Furio. Yes! Furio is there! We all loved it.

This guy is going to get exactly what he deserved. Do you know why? Because nobody fucks with Tony Soprano's best friend.

One of my other favorite scenes is when Tony and Furio speed up on his uncle's doctor's golf course in the middle of a game, almost running him over. Tony offers him a new golf club with a bow on it, which the doctor says he can't except.

"Well, I have one, and Mr. Williams here [Furio] doesn't play."

Furio says, "Stupida fuckin' game." He's upset that the doctor, who treated his uncle for cancer, was not returning his phone calls. Tony wants him to show him the respect he deserves. Furio keeps slowly moving towards the doctor, backing him up into a lake where his shoes end up in the water.

In an Italian accent, Furio calls out, "You got a bee on a you hat!" and smacks the guy's hat off into the water.

In a fantasy world, I think we all would secretly love to have these guys have our back. Just think, if you came across people that were causing you any real trouble in your life, Furio could always remind them that "there are worse things that could happen to a person then cancer."

I KNEW THE DAYS OF SEXUAL PLEASURE with this drug were over It looked like the paranoia was here to stay. It just wasn't worth it. I didn't think Billy thought it was worth it either. But knowing this still wasn't enough to keep me from giving in to the pull of the drug—so I decided to do it alone.

22

JOHN TRAVOLTA AND RADIO MAN

I FIRST SAW RADIO MAN, also known as Craig Castaldo, on the set of *I Am Legend*. I spotted an elderly man with semi-long gray hair and a long bushy beard. He had a radio tied around his neck on a thin rope. I thought maybe he was one of the main actors, hired to play a homeless man. I found out later that he wasn't *acting* like a homeless man, he *in fact was one at one time and certainly looked the part.*

Radio Man hung out around movie sets for years. He knew where and when they were filming and always showed up. Sometimes the cast and crews filming in New York City actually expected him to.

I saw him on several jobs. As time went on, I guess he started to make some money, because I noticed that the old beat-up radio around his neck had been replaced with a newer, better one.

Some people tried to talk to him. At times he was pleasant, but If he didn't feel like talking and wanted to be left alone, you would know it. He'd snap at you a little, and you would know to leave him alone. I didn't know his story; I also didn't know that he was a well-known fixture in New York City.

Apparently, Radio Man had come across the movie set of the movie *The Fisher King,* starring Robin Williams and Jeff Bridges. Robin Williams was amazed how much Radio Man resembled him, especially since his character in the movie was homeless. He even joked that maybe they were Siamese twins. Jeff Bridges also got to know him on the set.

After the very sad passing of Robin Williams, Jeff Bridges was doing a press conference for a new movie. He wanted to talk about his good friend and former co-star. He described a surreal encounter he had in Central Park with Robin Williams look-alike, Radio Man, the night before. He went on to described how he had been approaching his current-movie's party at the Central Park Boathouse. He was near the restaurant when he glanced out his car window and spotted Radio Man and momentarily mistook him for Robin.

He even turned to his wife and asked, "Is that Robin's ghost?"

When he realized it was Radio Man, it brought him back to all the great memories he'd had making the movie with Robin. He got out of the car and embraced Radio Man. He looked into his eyes and said, at that moment, he had truly felt Robin's spirit.

"HI, JOHN, YOU CALLED? HOW ARE YOU?"

"Good. Listen, you're finally going to get to see John Travolta. It's called *The Taking of Pelham 123*. I'm going to put you on the phone with Barbara. She's going to give you the instructions, you know, where and when. Just make sure you're on time. I have a couple of people going, so maybe you can all share a ride."

"Thanks, John! You're the *best!* This is going to be great! I *can't wait!*"

Our instructions were to wear winter clothes and dress in 1970s attire. They had beauticians there to straighten our hair, and extra clothes in case we didn't look authentic. The shoot was going to take place down in one of the New York City subways. We all had to wear winter coats, some with hats. There was just one thing—it was around 82° to 85°F. down in the subway, since it was summer. If it wasn't, it felt that way with all those clothes on. Shooting winter scenes in the summer is not fun. I didn't care, though—I was going to see John Travolta in person.

I waited there in my winter garb, sweat pouring down my face as if a shower was spraying on my head. One of the crew members asked me if I was okay, and if I wanted to leave and sit down somewhere.

"Nope, I'm fine. I'll be fine. I'm just a little hot."

Actually, I wasn't. I felt as if I was going to pass out, I was so hot.

Then all heads turned. . .*is* it? Can it *be*. . . ? I knew that walk anywhere. There he was—*John Travolta* in the *flesh!* I had to get the excess sweat out my eyes. I was probably close to fainting, but nothing was going to make miss seeing Vinnie Barbarino, Danny Zuko, and Tony Manero.

He looked great, even better in person. He was wearing all black and sporting a goatee. He shook a few hands—I guess he knew some of the people. I just stood there with my sweaty face in complete awe.

He did one scene, and then he was gone. *Is he coming out again? Wait!* He just passed me, he's walking up the subway stairs in front of me! He sees my friend, a seventy-year-old women named Tasha, walking up the stairs ahead of him. Tasha keeps up with all of us. Her biggest goal is to get to meet Denzel Washington. John Travolta takes her by the hand, walks on the side of her, and helps her up the subway stairs.

"Tasha," I said as I approached her. "Do you know who just helped you up those stairs?"

"No, who?"

"John Travolta!"

"No, it wasn't. Get out of here."

"Yes! Yes, it was! I was right behind you."

A big smile broke across her face. "Oh, Lord, I didn't even realize. Wow, John Travolta helped me up those stairs."

"Now you're probably going to meet Denzel today, too." We both started laughing.

"You know, I *luuuuv* my Denzel."

My friend Muriel and I were told to wait at a specific spot in the subway to do a scene. We had to do it a lot. I was really hot, so I snuck outside to get a little air once in a while. I had started seeing Billy again, and I'd been out with him the night before, so I hadn't gotten much sleep and my body wasn't in the best working order. Someone offered me something to eat, so I decided not to go back to my post right away, thinking it might make me feel better.

When I did return, Muriel said, "Don! Where *were* you?"

"Why? What happened?"

"*John Travolta* was here—I was just *talking* to him."

"What? What do you mean, talking to him?"

"He came over to do a scene and he started to talk to Radio Man."

I look around and sitting right there was Radio Man with his new radio around his neck. Muriel explained that, while they were talking, Radio Man jerked his head her way to signal John Travolta to talk to her. He introduced himself, as did she, and told him she was from Englewood, his hometown. She said he was really nice. They talked for a bit, and then he left.

"I was hoping you'd come back," she said. "Oh, Don, you missed it."

I can't help but wonder, if I hadn't been out with Billy the night before, basically contributing to the downfall of my life as I knew it, maybe I *would* have been there. I *know* I would have been there. You may think it was a small price to pay, that it didn't add up to much in the scheme of things. I happen to think that it's never a small price to pay when you miss an opportunity to meet John Travolta.

23

THE CALL

I WOKE UP EARLY ONE SUNDAY MORNING. I hadn't been able to find my cell phone again for a couple of days. It was dead, so I knew it was going to be hard to locate. I was so tired, up with the baby most of the night, but I had to find it. I went downstairs and started to search.

And there it was, of all places, under the couch. I plugged it into the charger and later saw that I had two missed calls from John. Oh, great, he must have had a job for me, I thought. He usually called me at least twice a week, but this was the first I've heard from him in a while.

I dialed my own number and put the proper code in to retrieve my messages.

"Hi, Don, it's John from Global. Guess what? You're going to be on *The Sopranos*. Call me back."

I just stood there for a second, waiting for the words to sink in. Then, a tremendous rush of joy came over me.

"Mom! *Mom!*" I went running in the kitchen. "Where

are you?" I heard her voice from afar.

"I'm down the basement doing laundry!" she shouted.

"What?"

"Come up, hurry up! I have to tell you something."

As she comes through the door, I shouted, "Guess what!"

"What, what?" she said, smiling.

"I'm going to be on *The Sopranos*. Can you *believe* it?"

"You're kidding," she said, flashing a big smile.

"John called and left the message on my machine. I have to call him back! I can't *believe* it!"

As I was dialing the number, my mother stood watching me. She didn't quite understand the urgency, and some might say my obsession with the show, but it kept my spirits up, and if I was happy, she was all for it.

"Hi, John, it's Don. I'm going to be on *The Sopranos?*"

"Yes! I promised I'd get you on, didn't I?"

"*Thank* you, John, *thank* you, *thank* you."

"You're welcome. Listen, I'm going to put you on the phone with Barbara—she'll give you all the details."

"Okay. *Thank* you, John, *thank* you. You're the *best!*"

"Okay, let me know how it goes."

I wrote down the information, hung up the phone, and began to call everyone that would be excited for me. It was so surreal. *Yes! I did it!*

I MUST SHARE YET ANOTHER STRANGE EXPERIENCE I had while writing this book. It happened while I was sitting at a table in my neighborhood library.

There were some days I would have doubts about

whether I could accomplish such a project, and that day happened to be one of them. Every time those thoughts came into my head—let's say I was driving at that moment—the song "Africa" would come on the radio. "High Hopes," sung by the group Panic! At the Disco was my inspirational song that came on exactly at the right time when a suspicion came into my head that my dream was unreachable. I felt something was telling me to do it, keep going. Was it the whispers Oprah talks about? Was it the universe? Maybe both. . .or maybe time to get my medication adjusted.

I was typing on the computer and happened to glance to the side of me where there were several round tables.

Oh, come on, no way! I thought. This is too much.

I swear to you, a guy who looked exactly like James Gandolfini was sitting right there.

I come from a small town, and you pretty much know all the usual faces, especially in the library. I had never seen that guy before.

I decided I was going to go over but not mention whom I thought he resembled.

"Hi, excuse me. Sorry to bother you. I was just wondering, do people think you look like any TV or movie actor?"

"Yes, he replied. "You know that actor, the mobster on TV, Tony Soprano?"

"You look just like him. Do you mind if I took a picture of you."

I wanted the picture in case anyone thought I was going completely nuts.

"Sorry, no, I don't think so."

I saw him sitting in the same spot a few times after that. I'd be typing each day and once in a while glance up, and there he was just sitting there. Then one day he was gone, and I haven't seen him since.

24

CRUTCH

I MET CRUTCH THROUGH BILLY and, as predicted, started meeting him on my own. He had one leg and walked with a crutch. I assumed that's how he got his nickname. I never really noticed because he would always pull up in his truck and I would walk up to him. I often wondered how he lost his leg. I would imagine a shooting or a gang fight, something like that. I never asked.

Something about him attracted me. He was a gangster type but in a cool way—very calm, if that makes any sense. He wasn't like other dealers who would ring your phone a couple of times and hang up to trigger your addiction. He would never rip you off, but if you got on his nerves, he would jerk your chain and annoy you as much as you did him.

Why always these bad boys and me? I guess it's their fearless way of going through life.

Crutch didn't take any shit from anyone. He had a way

about him that told you he wasn't afraid of anything. With a family to support, I guess he did what he did to survive or maybe just get the things he wanted. It wasn't as if he was selling to little kids on the street, just consenting adults. If it wasn't him, it would have been somebody else. I know, that's not a good way to rationalize, but how do you explain legalizing marijuana? Who cares who it hurts, it's revenue...and more than a tad hypocritical. One drug will lead to another, trigger depression, cause accidents. Other than for medical reasons, I think it's a big mistake.

I had a habit of calling way too many times when Crutch told me on more than one occasion not to. Once you put your order in, you must wait until they call you back. It could be an hour, could be two. I didn't listen, being under the influence already, and kept calling. After repeated defiance, Crutch often sent me on a wild goose chase to teach me a lesson.

He'd say he was going to meet me at a certain place, usually farther away than usual, then have me wait there for a good length of time.

"Crutch," I'd say on my cell, "where *are* you?"

"I'm here, don't you see me? Where you at?"

"Where? I can't see you. I'm on Grove."

"Drive down a couple of blocks to Hudson."

I would drive—it was more than a couple of blocks—park my car, and again look around. *Where is he!* Then my cell would ring. "I'm here—where you at? Hold on, I've got another call."

Finally, I thought. The waiting was killing me.

I'd be on hold for a good ten minutes. Then he'd come

back on the line and say, "Where were you? I was there. I didn't see you."

"What are you *doing*, Crutch? I was there, and you know it!"

"What the fuck you talking about? I don't have time for this shit."

"Where are you now?"

"On my way to the city."

"The *city*? Are you *kidding* me?"

I hung up the phone so *aggravated*. In my foggy state, I finally caught on as to what was going on. He had certainly gotten his point across. I was furious. He knew the best way to get back at a drug addict. It still didn't stop me from calling more than once when a lot of time had passed. At one time, he actually banned me from buying from them. Yes, they refused to sell to me. I was blacklisted for being too annoying.

One day, when I was meeting him, he pulled up with another guy in the car. "Don," he said, "I wanna introduce you to someone. This is Green. I'm going on a long trip. He'll be taking over for a while." I later figured out what the long trip was.

25

GREEN

GREEN WAS A GOOD-LOOKING, well-built Black man. I assumed his name came from the fact that he loved to make money; that was my take on it anyway. At first, he seemed excited and eager to get started on his new venture taking over the business, but he didn't know what he was in for. As time went by, he became hostile and stressed out, especially because my habit of calling did not stop. One day he met me in broad daylight, and from the look on his face, the stress the business put on him was evident. After all, he was dealing with a bunch of drug users looking for their next high.

"Don," he'd yell, "*look* at that parking job! Look at the way you're *parked*! Are you fuckin nuts? You don't think anyone would find that suspicious? Straighten up! You fucking *crazy*? There's something *wrong* with you."

It was during the day, and there were people all around, but he was the one yelling, drawing all this attention to us, worried about my parking job of all things.

When I first met Green, I believe I was in a black pantsuit and looking pretty good. It was when I first starting using. He was calm, all smiles, and seemed to be loving his new position. I really don't think he knew what he was in for, especially dealing with me.

One day months later, I met him to pick up. In exchange for extra, he needed me to drop him off somewhere. My hair was barely combed. I looked like a homeless person. My car was filthy, and I had totally forgotten I'd spilled something on the passenger's seat.

He sat down and was like, "What the *fuck!* It's all *wet!* Your car is a shithole. You need to clean this shit up! What's the matter with you?" He was clearly disgusted.

I could no longer take cash advances out on my credit card. I had no concept of how much I was charging, the penalties, or the consequences of my actions. I bought gift cards and sold them for cash. A guy someone hooked me up with bought them for a ten-dollar cut. Sometimes green would let me use them, if he was in a good mood.

I called him up one time, and he said no to the gift cards, cash only. I was desperate, I needed to get more, but how? He once told me out of anger that he would put me in one of those chain-gang rape things. I didn't care; my addiction was stronger than my fear. I told him I had the cash, so he sent someone to meet me. I took some Monopoly money, wet it and crumpled it up to make it look worn, then wrapped it around the gift card. In my mind, that was going to work: I was still *paying* him, just not the way he wanted.

I met the guy he sent, gave him the "trap," took the goods and got out of there. I had done it! Yes! I had pulled it off. I was amazingly calm—until *what* I'd done, and whom I'd *done* it *to*, sank in! Then I started to panic. Oh, shit...he's going to come *after* me!

The phone started to ring. It was Green. What was I going to *do?* I was acting like a chicken without a head, especially since I was coming down from my last high, which was never pleasant.

I found out he had told Billy. "Do you believe she gave me *Monopoly* money?" he said. "In the city, they will *shoot* you for that shit."

He told everyone that I'd still paid him with the card. But I guess he couldn't let it get out that he'd let me rob him completely, so, luckily, I got a pass.

26

FLAM

I LAID OFF GREEN FOR A WHILE after that anyway, because I knew there would be some sort of retaliation for my behavior. This could have included a full price for less than nothing on my next buy, or he could just have taken the money and given me nothing.

In came Flam. I remembered Billy dealing with him in the past. He used to call him from my phone, so I had his number.

Flam was a tall, slender Black man who looked like a throwback to the 1970s. He invariably dressed in colorful velvet attire, sporting a wide-rimmed black hat and a long jacket trimmed with fur. He looked like he'd just come off a movie set playing a pimp in one of the old movies. When he walked toward you, you'd swear you were in the '70s again, especially when he wore his purple bell-bottoms and gold chains around his neck.

It was never easy with Flam. When I called to buy from

him, he'd ask me to give him a ride somewhere that turned into a nerve-wracking experience. I just wanted to get my stuff and leave. He'd tell me that he needed to be dropped off at just "one place," but it would always turn into several.

"Flam, what are you doing? You said one place. I have to *go*."

"It's cool. . .it's cool," he'd say in his slow, calm voice. "I'll take good care of you."

"Flam, you always do this. . .this is the last place."

"For sure, for sure. I got you. . .don't worry, I got you."

Then the phone rang, and some guys would come outside. He'd get out, talk to them for a few minutes, and get back in.

"Flam I want no part of this. You need to get out." My nerves were shot by then.

"Just one more stop, Don, one more."

We pulled up to another curb, and now two guys were getting *into* the car. "They just need a ride up the street, Don, just up the street."

"Flam, you do this *every time!*"

He did his business with them while we are driving, collecting money and passing goods, as I thought, Get me the hell *out* of here—a cop car's going to pull us over any minute, and I'm going to *jail*. I have become an accessory to a dealer. How did I get *into* this?

Down the block turned out to be fifteen minutes away. "Flam, you're getting out with them. That's *it!*"

"That's cool, that's cool."

I pulled over and the guys got out. I gave him the money for my stuff. He handed it to me and was about to leave.

"Flam," I said, "what about the extra?"

He reached in his pocket and handed me a little bag with something that looked like a tiny little pebble.

"That's *it?*" I said. "Are you *kidding* me?"

"...Well, if you give me a ride to this place, I can get you some more."

"Forget it. For*get* it, Flam. *Goodbye!*"

He finally gets out, thank God! I'm soaked with sweat and my nerves are completely shot. I grew up in a good family; now I'm driving around with drug dealers. If we got stopped, that's *it* for me. They tap phones all the time. I always say, the next morning, that I'm done. But then I'm out there seeking it again. I should never have alienated Green with my Monopoly money, but that's water under the bridge.

After that night, contacting Flam becomes strictly a last resort. I cannot trust a word he says.

That's funny—did I really think I could trust the word of a *drug dealer?*

27

LUCKY

LUCKY WAS A YOUNG GUY—I don't know exactly how young, maybe twenty-five. He was a tall and well-built man like, as you may have noticed from reading this, a lot of dealers. He was funny and seemed to get a kick out of me. He mentioned he had a young son. He wasn't with his "baby mama," as he put it, but he would see his son often.

He got his name because I couldn't think of it when I wrote down his number, so I put it under "Lucky" in my phone contacts. I also thought it was a good name to keep me from getting caught. It stuck, so that's what I took to calling him. I had a CD in my car of Jason Mraz, one of my favorite artists, that I listened to all the time. It had a song called "Lucky," so I played it for him and told him it was his song. He laughed.

I had met him, as I had the others, through Billy. He was seeing this girl; and lived in motels and spent their days dealing.

One thing about doing drugs: When you're high and you want more, you will promise almost anything to get some. The dealer will take advantage of that. If you want credit for a fifty, he would only give you twenty dollars' worth, but you still owed fifty the next day. But twenty wouldn't be enough, so if they gave you credit for fifty, you would owe them a hundred. You didn't care at the time, though; you just wanted *more*. In the course of the night, you could rack up a pretty hefty bill. By the next day, you could wake up owing maybe two hundred and fifty to three hundred dollars—and you'd better have it.

I saw Lucky's other side first-hand one day. He wanted me to drop him off somewhere, but of course he lied. The next thing I knew, he made me park outside a house. Then he dialed a number on his cell phone. "Where's my *money?*" he shouted into it. "...I don't *give a shit!* I want my money *now!* . . . I'm right outside. Get your fucking ass out here *now!*"

Lucky, the sweet guy with the nicest smile, had turned into a heartless prick screaming at a guy, whom I could hear whine on the phone in this pitiful, almost tearful voice, "I don't have it, man. I'll get it, I'm sorry, I'll get it. I *promise* I'll *get* it. My grandma is here. I don't have it."

Lucky's screams got louder.

"Stop, Lucky!" I snapped. "*Stop!* Get out of my car."

"You told me last *night* you had it. . .I'm going to drag your ass out of that fucking house. You better have it by tomorrow, or I'm coming back for *your ass!*"

"I will, I will."

The poor guy sounded like he was in tears.

I said, "You're an asshole, Lucky! What are you doing?"

"Hey, he said he would have the money *today*."

"You asked him while he was high. What did you expect? He was going to tell you *anything*. Don't pretend you're stupid, Lucky, you knew exactly what you were doing. That's how you all make your money."

"I didn't want to knock on his door and upset his grandmother and all."

"How nice of you," I said sarcastically. "You upset *me!* Don't get me *involved* in this shit. Is this the kind of person you want to be? Do you feel good about yourself? That was disgusting."

I saw the look on Lucky's face after that. I knew this wasn't him. He did feel badly. I didn't know much about Lucky's past. He cared about his son, that I knew. What had led him to this kind of life?

I spoke to him about it years later, when he was no longer in the game. I told him I was proud of him, and that he could do much more with his life.

He said, "You know, you were the only one who said that, the only one who was actually happy for me."

28

IT'S CALLING MY NAME

WHEN I FIRST STARTED USING DRUGS, it would only be when I was with Billy, which was once in a while. But when I started using on my own, things began to go downhill. I no longer had control of my behavior, falling deeper and deeper into addiction. Every morning, after feeling like death, paying double on credit, lending my apartment out for several nights, I still woke up and ended up seeking more.

It was like driving to one place with good intentions and somehow, without being fully conscious of what I was doing, winding up at a friend's house to borrow money, or to a store to return something—as if something was taking over my mind.

We have all driven in a car and gone into a deep daze and somehow arrived where we were going. A part of our brain was driving the car; and the other was in la-la land. That's the best way I can describe my experience.

It reminds me of an episode of *The Sopranos* called "*Long Term Parking.*" Silvio, played by the multi-talented Steven Van Zandt, is supposed to be picking up Adriana, played by Drea de Matteo, to see Christopher in the hospital. In one scene, you see her at the wheel, driving alone, with her red suitcase resting on the seat next to her, heading towards Baltimore. You then see the scene switch to her in the passenger seat, with Silvio driving. I think her instincts have always told her that she should leave Christopher and get away from the dangerous life of organized crime. I'm sure she would always try to build up the courage.

On that day, in my opinion, once again that was her intention—to get away. Her addiction to Christopher and the life he led was too strong...which ultimately led to her demise.

Her face is still bruised by Christopher; Sil begins to make small talk, assuring her that Christopher is going to be alright. After a while, she happens to look up and notices they are driving through a wooded area. She starts to realize what is happening. She says nothing, but the tears start streaming down her face. What happens next is one of the most shockingly surprising, realistic, heartbreaking scenes I have ever seen. Just her last thoughts of how Christopher betrayed her are enough to bring tears to your eyes. Although I have read it was a tough scene for Mr. Van Zandt to play, the performance by these two actors was phenomenal.

It took me some time to get over that scene. I'm sure I'm not the only one who was affected. After all...we loved Adriana.

THERE ARE MANY KINDS OF ADDICTIONS—food, shopping, and gambling to name a few. With them come triggers, which are certain people places and things you should avoid. When it comes to drugs, alcohol is one of these triggers. My one night out with Dana proved this to be true.

Dana was very busy; I always wanted to spend more time with her, so she saw me as much as she could. One thing remained a certainty—she took me out to eat every year for my birthday. We met at one of our favorite spots. It was a night I looked forward to, and she knew it.

We ordered a couple of drinks and had some food...but after the second drink, I no longer wanted to be there. My whole mindset seemed to change. I went to the ladies' room and made a phone call. It was not my plan, especially since we had only been out for a short time.

"Dana," I said when I got back to the table, "I think I'm going to go—I don't really feel that good."

"You're going to go *now*? We just *got* here. No you're not, you're staying."

"No, really, I don't feel good."

"...Who are you meeting? I know you're meeting somebody. Billy?"

"No one, I swear. I'm sorry. Thanks for dinner...I had fun."

Dana was not stupid. She had suspected for months that I was up to something, but not a hundred percent sure.

When I asked to borrow money, supposedly for gas, she would say okay but not give me cash. If I wanted it, I would have to follow her to the gas station, and they would put it on her credit card.

"Why do I have to follow you? Why can't you just give me the money? That is so ridiculous."

"Because I'm not giving you cash. If you want the gas, I'll just follow you. What's the big deal?"

I usually got very annoyed. Being a nurse, though, Dana could read the signs of addiction, though, until she was positive, she wasn't going to act on it. I was not a very good friend to her during this period of my life. If you're an addict, you're not a good anything to anybody.

We left the restaurant and went our separate ways. I felt badly because she looked really hurt. Things that had been crucially important to me weren't anymore. I was just a shell of what I had been, controlled by a force I couldn't stop. I knew it was deadly, but I went ahead and sank my teeth into the forbidden fruit. You would think we'd all have learned from Adam and Eve.

Not all of us.

29

DOWN FOR THE COUNT

I WENT UP TO MY DOOR and called Lucky. He let me in. Just then the phone rang. It was Dana, who had been right behind me but hadn't seen me. "Don, what is *wrong* with you? I'm outside. Open the door."

"Dana! No, I don't feel good, I'm going to sleep."

"Let me *in!* What is going *on?*"

I hung up the phone or thought I did. The doorbell started to ring over and over, but I ignored it—my mind was only on one thing. Lucky and I went in the bedroom, and he handed me a little piece of paper. I opened it and saw that there was very little of what I wanted in it.

"That's *it?*" I said. "For *three nights?*"

"*Four* nights," he said, and that he would "take care of me" the next day.

"That's a rip-off, Lucky. You said three nights on the phone, and that you had plenty to give me."

"Well, you're not getting more now. I don't have it.

Maybe later."

"You're such a liar, Lucky, like always. Why didn't you tell me that on the phone? This is bullshit! I want more than this."

"I told you, I *don't have it!* Hit me up later."

I kept arguing with him but settled in the end for what he gave me.

I had no idea that Dana heard the whole thing—the conversation, the argument, *everything*.... I'd left the line open, so it hadn't disconnected. She immediately called my family and told them everything.

I LEFT MY APARTMENT, STILL VERY ANNOYED with Lucky, and headed to my usual bar to get a couple of drinks before I got high. I reached my mother's house about an hour and a half later and walked in to find Big Dog, my other brother Garrett, and my mother standing in the living room, staring at me as if they'd just been to a funeral—although, now that I think of it, Big Dog looked more like a boiling, covered pot, steaming and on the verge of blowing any minute.

"What have you been *doing?*" he said in a stern, loud voice.

I looked at my mother. Her face was full of anguish and on the verge of tears.

"What.... What?" I started toward the kitchen.

"*Get In Here!*" he barked, slow and curt.

He was furious. Garret was the calm brother. He stood there quietly, just taking it all in, probably hoping he was watching a bad movie he'd happened to switch on at three o'clock in the morning.

I said, "Okay, wait a minute. I have to go to the bathroom. I will be right there."

I must have been truly messed up, because I can't believe what I did next. I locked the bathroom door, pulled my pants down, sat on the seat, and proceeded to light up my pipe.

The next thing I knew, Boom! Big dog *knocked in the door.* What a sight that must have been. I remember him grabbing my arm and pulling me hard off the seat.

The next memory I have is of somehow getting past him and my brother Garrett, and going out the door. But instead of going straight to the second door leading outside, I made a left to the door leading to the inside porch, ran through and exited to the outside porch, and leaped to the ground. I ran toward the highway and, somehow, made it the ten blocks back to my apartment. I got there and started ringing the doorbell furiously, and rapidly pounding the door in an utter panic.

"Lucky, Lucky! Let me in...*Lucky!*"

30

THE TEST DREAM

WE ALL HAVE HAD CRAZY DREAMS. What do they mean? In the *Sopranos* episode called "The Test Dream," Tony, separated from Carmela, stays at the Plaza Hotel in New York City. After a tryst with a prostitute, he falls asleep alone while watching a movie. The stresses of being The Boss become inadvertently incorporated into a dream.

He awakes, so he thinks, next to the deceased New York don Carmine Lupertazzi (played brilliantly by the late Tony Lip), who informs Tony that there is nothing on the other side and tells him to speak to God on the phone. (God's voice is played by the *legendary creator of The Sopranos,* David Chase.)

When things weigh on your mind, they make their way into your dreams. This episode was praised by a lot of professionals, mainly analysts. Many concluded that people, and situations, were causing Tony Soprano way too much stress. Although they were, or needed to be, removed permanently, it was not something he wanted to do but knew ultimately had to be done. I assume his cousin Tony B. would be the hardest. Though he was saving him from a *tortuous* death, shooting him point plank in the chest had to be a near rock-bottom task, even for Tony Soprano.

Anything can happen in a crazy dream. Tony fires a gun and discovers that the bullets are made of feces. Hence, his speech: "I'm like King Midas in reverse—everything I touch turns to shit."

The dream continues. Meeting Finn's parents is wild, because his mother was played by actress Annette Benning. While all the parents are at the dinner table, getting to know one another, Tony leans toward her and says, "Hey, you're Annette Benning."

It's great when you discover that you are really dreaming, as Tony does.

This dream sequence reminds me of some of my background jobs that seemed like a dream but were actually happening. I was on the set of *Rescue Me* once. It was time for the lunch break, and all the extras were in a little room eating on long commissary tables. We were invariably separated from the major stars. I was sitting with my friend Marina when I looked up and saw a woman. "Marina," I said, "see the girl sitting over there? She looks like Tatum O'Neil".

She looked over and very calmly said, "That's because it *is* Tatum O'Neil."

An Academy Award-winning actress just sitting there eating with the rest of us! I kept looking over, and yes, it was her. I wanted to go over and say hello, but I didn't. Am I dreaming this? I wondered. I'm eating with Tatum O'Neill. What a talent. I always hoped that, one day, *her* Quentin Tarantino would come along.

Another far-out, dreamlike situation was meeting John Bobbitt's ex-sister-in-law on one of the background jobs. She was young, blonde, flirty, very friendly, and filled with energy. Hanging with her was a lot of fun.

John Bobbitt, you may recall, got his penis cut off by his wife Lorena in 1993. It made the news all over the world. It was shocking that a woman would actually do such a thing. She claimed he had sexually and physically abused her.

The ex-sister-in-law went on to tell me what a nice guy John really was and wanted to set me up with him.

"Really?" I told her, smiling. "That's okay. Thank you, but I think I'm going to have to pass."

She laughed. "He really is a nice guy. Leave a message—I know he'll like you."

She dialed his number and put her phone up to my ear, so I could hear his machine: *Hi, this is John. Leave your name and number.*

I moved back quickly, and we both started laughing. "Really," I said, "I'm good."

Some of my realities being an extra *could* feel like a crazy dream.

31

VIRAL SPIRAL

Lucky swings open the door. "Shit! What's the matter with you, girl?" I was still hysterical from running ten blocks back to my apartment and frantically ringing the doorbell and pounding on the door.

"Lucky, let me in! *You have to let me in!* My family is after me. I have to *hide*. My friend told them *everything*."

"Hell, no, you're not coming in here."

"What do you mean, I'm not coming in? It's *my* apartment! Lucky. . .*please.*"

"Not *tonight* it isn't. Sorry, Don, you're on your own. I'm with my girl, and three's a crowd—you know what I'm sayin'?"

I just stare at him with tears in my eyes. "Thanks a *lot*, Lucky." I turn away.

"You'll be all right," I hear from a distance.

I'm still numb from all the things I have been doing tonight, but not enough to feel abandoned by Lucky. He's always been very nice to me, except when we argued. He did what he did, but he had a good head on his shoulders. I knew eventually he would choose a different path. I always thought that on some level he cared for me, too, for people. He wasn't cut out for the kind of life he was leading; he didn't have the heart for it. I saw the guilt on his face when he profited from people's addictions. He tried to be an unfeeling badass, but it was starting to take its toll on him.

Regardless, he'd given me my walking papers. I started to head back toward the main road. I had no idea where to go or what I was doing.

Alone in the dark, I heard loud rock music in the distance behind me. It got closer and louder. A car pulled up next to me. It was Lucky and his girlfriend. "Come on. Watch you *waiting* for? Get *in!*"

I smiled and jumped in. The radio was still playing an epic song when Lucky leaned over and handed me a flask of tequila. We all talked and laughed and rode around, but I knew it was the end of the line for me.

In a way, I was relieved. It was over, and I was ready to face the music. I just wanted to escape with them for a short time and forget about everything.

After a while, I knew what I had to do. "Lucky, can you drop me off at my mom's?"

32

THE SOPRANOS

I COULD HARDLY SLEEP the night before, knowing that the next day I was actually going to be an extra on *The Sopranos*. Was it really happening? The instructions were to dress up in a pair of pajamas, slippers, and a bathrobe. We were going to be playing mental patients. Our hair was to look unkempt, and we were to wear no makeup.

I went to the store beforehand and spent a couple of hours trying to find the perfect pair of pajamas. I wanted to look nice. I settled on a silky pink pair with flowers and a matching robe. I found out my friend Marina had been called as well.

The destination was a real hospital in New Jersey. We had to report to a room to fill out our paperwork. Marina and I were soon sitting in a rather small room with a bunch of extras from other agencies. We had no makeup on, messy hair, and our pajamas in a bag, waiting for the word to get dressed.

As I was looking around the room, checking everyone out, it dawned on me that they were dressed a lot differently. They had on nice clothes, high heels, and their hair done nicely, with full makeup on.

"Marina, why are we the only ones that look like this?"

"I don't know—maybe we should ask somebody."

I hurried up to one of the people in charge and asked them how we were supposed to be dressed. It turned out that we had received the wrong information. We were supposed to be in nice attire, with full makeup and neat hair. We were supposed to be the *visiting parents* of patients, not the patients themselves.

"Oh, no, are you *kidding* me? . . . Marina, what are we going to do? These are the only clothes I brought. I can't believe this. I worked so hard to get here."

I felt my eyes start to tear up. She could see I was getting upset. But I remembered I had left some clothes in my car from a previous extra job, so I dashed out to see what I could find.

I found an old-looking black jacket, very wrinkled, but I figured it was better than what I had on. I went to the bathroom and tried to fix my hair, which was hard because I'd put a lot of hairspray on to make it stick up. I used the only few pieces of makeup that I brought—a little liner and lipstick. I still didn't look great, but I hoped it would give me a chance.

I found out later that it was the follow-up episode after AJ, played by Robert Idler, Tony's young son, tries to commit suicide. He ties a brick to his leg and jumps in the family pool. Thank God Tony happens to be walking in the door and hears AJ's cries from the backyard. He's puzzled about what's going on until he realizes and jumps in the pool to help him.

That scene was brilliant and moving. It brought me to tears. The acting that came out of those two stars was riveting. Robert Idler mirrored the struggles of depression without missing a beat. Of course, the brilliant writers deserve the credit as well. James Gandolfini's acting—what can I say, was emotionally powerful and truly authentic.

As we were waiting, a young girl came into the room. She wasn't feeling well and really didn't want to be there. She got picked to play one of the hospitalized kids. She told us they had her pretend to yank out a strand of her hair, looking troubled of course. I later saw it when the episode aired.

They finally came and got us. The anticipation was over. We were told to line up on both sides of a long hallway, most everyone in nice clothes and high heels, looking good. I didn't—my jacket was wrinkled, I had jeans on, and I was wearing sneakers. I looked like an unmade bed. Two people came walking up and down the long lines, checking us out. I tried to move forward away from the wall, so I could be noticed. Underneath, I was thinking, Please pick me. I didn't mean to dress like this. I don't really consider this nice attire. After the third walk-by, they started pointing to people. I wasn't one of them. A woman announced that, if you hadn't been picked, you could go back to the holding room, and then she thanked us.

I saw Marina walking back as well. I had no words to say. I went into the hallway outside the holding room and sat by myself. I called my mother and told her what had happened. I'd come so close. I felt horrible. All I could do is sit there. I started to feel my eyes tearing up.

"Stop!" I said to myself.

But I couldn't stop—the tears just kept streaming out of my eyes. I thought, with all the problems in the world, I'm going to fall apart because my biggest crisis is not appearing on *The Sopranos*. What's the matter with me? Was all this really about getting a picture with him to fulfill a crazy obsession? Crazy or not, it didn't matter—I felt like shit. As I sat in the hallway wallowing in self-pity, Marina came out and spotted me. "Don, Don, hurry! Come here! I found out that James Gandolfini goes into the hospital kitchen to get his food. One of the extras saw him in there.

". . .What kitchen? Are we allowed in there?"

"Yes, I'll show you. Hang out in there," she said with excitement in her voice. Maybe you'll get to see him."

We went through a couple of doors and found ourselves in the small hospital kitchen. It was stocked with every kind of dessert you can think of, top of the line. There were also a lot of pasta dishes and deli meats to make any kind of sandwich that fit your mood. There were all kinds of coffee and tea as well.

Some of the extras came in to get some food and went back to the holding room. I stalled and took my time, pretending that I was deciding what I wanted. I left and came back in fifteen minutes to get myself a cup of tea— that was my story anyway.

I found myself alone in the room, in the corner, dunking my tea bag in the hot water. I had been dunking it for the last twenty minutes, hoping James Gandolfini would come in. Nobody was in the room but me. As I stood there hypnotized by the steam of the tea, the door swung open. I look up, and *there he was!* My eyes, my body, my mind, couldn't believe what they were seeing. He was so *tall*. His presence filled the room. Bigger than life.

"Time to eat," he said as he grabbed a plate.

He was gathering his food when some other people came into the room. I was dying to say something to him, but we had been told that we couldn't. They were working and wanted an atmosphere with no fans interested in pictures or autographs. It had to be professional. I had to say something to him, though—if I didn't, I know I would regret it.

He had a lot of things in both hands to bring out to where he was going, and it looked like he was struggling, so I walked up to him and said the stupidest thing: "Can I hold it for you?"

Hold what? It reminds me of what Baby said to Johnny in *Dirty Dancing* saying, "I carried a watermelon." How stupid.

He just looked at me with a half smirk and went on his way. Some extras I have come across can be rather strange; maybe he thought I was one of them. I laugh about it now, but of all things to say, really.

I WAS CUTTING A GUY'S HAIR years later and told him the story of my encounter. He said that he'd served food on the

Sopranos set for a couple of years. He said that Mr. Gandolfini usually stays in character on set. Come to think of it, that was a Tony Soprano look if you ask me.

From then on, they left the other kitchen door open that led out to the hallway where they were shooting the scenes. It was perfect. I just hung out in the kitchen, browsing around the food, pretending to be fixing yet another cup of tea. Glancing out into the hallway, I saw the actor who played AJ in a hospital gown. He was so friendly. He smiled and said hello to me. Between takes, he'd walk down the hallway and chat with James Gandolfini. I felt as if I was watching an episode of *The Sopranos* right in front of my eyes. It looked like AJ was talking to his father, when, in reality, it was just two great actors shooting the breeze. It was incredible.

I've always had the ability to blend in and look like I belong. I knew they didn't want anyone hanging out in the kitchen. I stayed because I knew I had this special quality. At one point, I actually leaned against the doorway and watched everything that was going on. I just acted like I belonged, and nobody questioned me—they never do.

Am I here? Is this real? Am I really seeing this? Believe me, when you actually see a star you've admired for so long right in front of you, it doesn't seem real.

There was a boom box in the hallway. They started to play a really good song that I don't recall knowing, very loud. I now know the scene they were shooting. While the music plays, Tony bursts out of the double doors of the hospital. The music that made it onto show was different from the one they were playing then. It was the final scene of the episode.

By then, word got out of my scene-watching escapade. More and more extras started gathering in the kitchen. Then in came a really nasty girl, "Okay, everyone," she barked. "Clear out of here—you're not supposed to be in here!"

Shit, I thought, *they blew my cover.* I followed everybody out, and thought I would wait a little while and then try to make my way back in. I knew they were almost done, so I was hoping to achieve my ultimate goal if, maybe, I could catch him alone in the kitchen.

A woman came in, thanked us, and said we were done for the day. A line formed, and everyone began getting signed out. As soon as I was done, I headed for the kitchen. But when I walked in, there she was, the witch on wheels. "Didn't I tell you to stay out of here?"

Where's the respect for non-union extras. We are an important piece of every movie and TV show. Without us, they couldn't be made. Everyone else was nice on the *Sopranos* set. Some people treat you well, and some like third-class passengers on the *Titanic.* Still, in all fairness, she was only doing her job.

I didn't get a picture with the great James Gandolfini, but it was a day in my life that was truly, amazingly unforgettable.

33

DIVINE INTERVENTION

Lucky and his girlfriend dropped me off at my mom's house. I knew what was waiting for me. I was numb because of the liquor I'd consumed, so I wasn't scared. In a way, I remember feeling relieved. I wanted it to be over. I knew I couldn't stop on my own.

When you're in that state of mind, you have no regard for how your actions will affect other people, including the ones you love most. You disregard people who have helped you your whole life, loved you, dedicated their life to your happiness, in the worst way. In my case, my mother was the worst casualty.

I made my way up her stairs, barely, and let myself in. They were all still there and looked my way as I entered. My mom's face was filled with anguish.

"Come on, we're taking you to a hospital," Big Dog said in a clear, stern voice.

"I'll be alright. Not tonight. I'm tired, I'll go

tomorrow."

The next thing I recall is two police officers walking through the door. "Come on, Ms. We're going to get you some help."

I was so out of it but then realized that they were coming toward me. I pictured myself writing a movie script. If I was writing that scene, I thought, if I was to stand there calmly and say, "Okay, put the restraints on me, let's go," it would look stupid. I felt, in my disoriented state, that I had to resist. When you're going to be taken to a mental ward, you don't just stand there and say "Okay, let's go." So I put up a fight. . .not cool. The whole scene was embarrassingly humiliating and so not cool, especially coming from a small town.

It reminded me of yet another great episode of *The Sopranos* called "The Strong, Silent Type." That episode was brilliantly written and acted. It included Christopher's intervention (played wonderfully by Michael Imperioli) organized by family and friends. Interventions are the last resort for families and loves ones when someone is abusing drugs.

Often people who are doing something unhealthy, when you confront them, will try to turn the light onto *you* and *your* downfalls: "Well, *you* do things that are not good for you. Don't judge *me!*"

Christopher reached that point when each of his friends took turns describing his behavior during his highs. With a trained counselor present trying to keep things in check, everyone took turns explaining how his drug use had affected his—and their—lives in a destructive and negative way.

Adriana revealed that they had once made love every night, but that, since he started getting high, he could no longer function as a man. It was also revealed that he accidentally fell asleep and suffocated her small dog, which enraged Tony.

"You killed little Cosette? I oughtta suffocate *you*, you little prick!"

Of course, this just opened the wounds of losing his pet horse, Pie-O-My, due to Ralphie. I'm sure some animal rights activists were not shedding a tear over what happened to *him* after that.

Silvio said that he'd come into the club early one morning to find Christopher's head half in the toilet. Carmela (played by the amazingly talented Edie Falco) pointed out that he'd been high at her mother-in-law's wake, and Paulie just told him he was weak, out of control, and an embarrassment to himself and everyone else.

Christopher then turned the tables: "He who is without sin, let him cast the first stone" was his mindset. He spoke about the lack of self-control all of them suffered from— Sil sleeping with women with a wife and kids at home, bringing up the Russian incident with Paulie, and ultimately disrespecting Tony.

Paulie (The Great Tony Sirico) got up and grabbed him by the shirt. His mother yelled, "Good, maybe someone will smack some God damn sense into him!"

"Great, my own mother. Fuck *you!* You fuckin' *whore!*" That was *it*: All the guys got up and proceeded to beat him up and send him to the hospital.

To me, it was a classic wise guy intervention. It was very realistic and extremely entertaining, one of my favorites.

This scene did highlight, though, the behavior of a person addicted to drugs. Many people in that room could have ended his life at any time, yet he resisted and disrespected all of them, especially Tony, who was the boss. If it hadn't been for Tony, Christopher would have been dead a long time before. So he had no choice. It was either rehab or swim with the fishes.

It was hard for Christopher to stay clean in that line of work. Drinking acted like a trigger, and the crew mostly hung out at a bar. Christopher tried to limit his time there, but then started to feel out of the loop. His friends wanted the old Christopher back. They thought he was cured and should have self-control and be able to handle a couple of drinks.

But everyone in recovery knows: Sometimes it only takes that one drink.

I DIDN'T HAVE A TRAINED COUNSELOR on hand, and people didn't go down the line and say their peace. I knew I would lose everything, however, if I didn't get help—everything meaning my daughter. Christopher knew it would be his life. Sometimes a good incentive leads you in the right direction.

I am here to tell you that you must listen and do whatever it takes to keep moving in that direction. If you fall, get up, pray, listen, and try again. You can do it, with the help of God. I know you can do it.

34

ROCK BOTTOM

AFTER THAT MOST HUMILIATING SCENE, I was transported to the infamous Bergen Woods, which was known to almost everyone as the place you went when you, well, lost your marbles, so to speak. When I volunteered on the local ambulance corps, we use to take a lot of people up there. I never thought that, one day, I would actually be a patient. I didn't think a lot of things.

Big Dog, along with my family, soon joined me. Karen showed up as well. They tried to convince the doctors that I was a danger to myself, so that I would be committed to a hospital and get the help I needed. I, on the other hand, tried to talk the doctors out of it, downplaying my situation. Dana had to go out of town or she would have been there, but told them what to say and do. Thank God she did.

I wound up being transferred, anxiety ridden, to a very cold, unpleasant facility. Because I was on medication, it had to be a psychiatric ward. It didn't help that I could hear patients clearly out of control, crying, yelling, or slamming things around. No phone calls or visitors for forty-eight hours, and no televisions in the rooms: What a nightmare.

One of my big anxiety issues was not being able to leave a place if I wanted to. Throughout my life, I had to take my own car places, hardly ever planned long vacations, and rarely went on family road trips. I couldn't feel trapped. I had to be able *to get out of there.*

I didn't need a psychiatrist to tell me where that came from. I had been trapped in school every day, always in fear. Almost every day, I had been stuck in a volatile situation. I felt it in the psychiatric facility, too. *I can't stand it!* my mind shrieked. *I have to get out!*

35

HOLSTEN'S

Rumor has it that the last episode of *The Sopranos* was going to be filmed at an ice-cream parlor in Bloomfield, New Jersey, called Holsten's. You *know* I had to go down there. I just wanted to be a part of the excitement. I wasn't working, so I was free to ask for a picture if the opportunity presented itself.

Really, let it go already, I thought. There will be tons of people there and probably no chance.

That thought didn't stop me from bringing my plastic disposable camera, just in case.

My mom agreed to watch my daughter. I showed up at Holsten's to find the streets packed with tons of *Sopranos* fans. The air was filled with excitement as camera crews and news media swarmed the area. As I walked around taking it all in, I ran into the same nice guy who owned a costume store I had just visited. I'd put down a deposit on two costumes for my daughter's first birthday party the following week, a bunny and a dinosaur.

"Hey, how's it going?" he asked.

"Isn't this exciting? I can't believe all these people are here."

He introduced me to a young couple who had been cast to sit in one of the booths in Holsten's for one of the last scenes.

"You guys are so lucky!" I said

They were very nice and very excited. Who wouldn't have been?

I was strolling around through the crowd when I came upon a very tall, muscular man looking as if he was a bodyguard of some sort. "Excuse me," I asked, "are you on Mr. Gandolfini's security team?"

I think he said he was some kind of security for him. It was so loud I couldn't hear.

"If he comes out," I said, "can you ask him if I could get a quick picture with him? Please—it would mean so much to me."

He shook his head. "You're going to have a hard time getting any kind of pictures with this big a crowd. Your best bet is going down the block by the trailers."

I didn't see any trailers in the near distance, and I didn't want to leave and miss anything. I stood there for a bit more before I noticed a bunch of people running really fast down the block. Without thinking, I crossed the street and started running with them. They were going at a pretty fast pace. I had one of those Big Gulp sodas in one hand and my camera in the other, and my sweatpants started to fall as I ran. Trying to prevent myself from being exposed, I held the plastic camera under my arm and pulled each side up as I kept up the pace.

A long block and a half later, I realized I was running with a bunch of reporters. They'd just gotten word James Gandolfini and Edie Falco were going to pose for a picture.

I put down my Big Gulp by a tree and joined the reporters. Even without a professional camera, no one questioned me.

The rest of the crowd was secured out of the area by the police. I remember hearing a guy yell, "No one can tell me that I can't be on my property."

At that point, I got a bit nervous, clearly being where I didn't belong.

I was still standing there when a man appeared before us. He said he was going to allow one picture of James and Eddie together on the condition that we would not call any other type of media to come down.

They walked out and posed arm in arm like Tony and Carmela. I took out my camera, lifted it, and started snapping along with the rest of the reporters. All I could hear was constant clicking. Thank God it was noisy, because no one could hear the sounds my camera was making between pictures. It would have blown my cover.

It's official, I suppose—I am a complete nut! But I got a great picture! *John is going to love it too*, I told myself. *It's going to look great hanging on the agency wall. I may not have gotten the picture I wanted, but I think now I can put my little obsession to rest.*

It was time to go home to my daughter.

The crowd soon began to disperse, and I began to head

back up the street as well, to where my car was parked. Thirsty from all that running, I realized I had forgotten my Big Gulp, and had doubled back to the tree to get it, when I saw James Gandolfini. He was walking right toward me and seemed to be in a rush. I stopped walking, and he looked over at me.

Awe-struck, I said, "Hi—can I just get a picture with you?"

"I'm really sorry. I can't right now," he said, walking swiftly past me.

I had been playing a reporter not too long before, I told myself, and he might've recognized me. Taking a picture with a woman might not be a good idea for a celebrity either, especially the way the media works.

But, looking back, I wish I had said more. In fact, I should have said more. I should have told him how much it meant to me and what lengths I had gone to. I know he would have done it then. He is known to have been a kind, sweet, giving person to everyone but he was in a rush and shooting the last scene of the last episode. It obviously wasn't a good time. I'd gotten a great picture earlier, not the one I had hoped for, regardless I was still very happy. It was an exciting day, and I was so glad to be a part of it.

I walked up the street to where my car was parked. It was time to go home to my daughter.

36

OUT OF THE FOG

AFTER A VERY LONG FIVE-DAY STAY, I was finally allowed to come home. There was a condition: I had to attend an outpatient facility. I had agreed to do so, and it turned out to be the best thing for me. Everything they taught me about addiction was a hundred percent true. There were people of all ages, races, and classes. Addiction does not discriminate.

I learned so much from my stay there, especially from the people. Their stories were all different but had led them to the same result. The counselors seemed to know exactly what we were going through. A lot of them, I learned, had experienced addiction first-hand or been close to someone who had.

The drug has a mind of its own. I got a taste of how truly powerful it was when I had just finished my treatment. I came home to find an old garbage bag in the bathroom that was not yet full. Without a thought or realizing what

I was doing, I began rummaging through it, trying to find a piece I might have left behind months before.

It was like I blacked out for a minute. What are you *doing?* I asked myself. It was as if something else had been temporarily controlling me. . .knowing that bag could be there was a *trigger*. I couldn't believe how right they had been at the facility. Unbelievable. Luckily, there was nothing in it.

The outpatient rehab had people who came on their own, but some were court ordered. There was a guy that I used to see outside, smoking, during one of our breaks. He reminded me so much of Crutch. He had a tough exterior but a Marlon Brando voice. I asked him once how he was holding up. I'll never forget his response. Looking down, soberly shaking his head back and forth, he said, "I don't know . . .it's calling my name."

37

SATIN DOLLS

THE *SOPRANOS* FINALE WAS ON! I was *so* excited. I thought the best place to watch it would be Satin Dolls, aka The Bada Bing. I was sure they'd have something going on. Who could I get to go with me? Most of my friends were married by then and wouldn't be allowed to go to a strip club—including my brothers.

My friend Mitch! That's who I'll call. He was my friend's boyfriend. They'd had a child together, and I knew she would be cool with it. I knew I would have a good time with him, too.

Mitch hadn't been brought up in a *Leave It to Beaver* family as I had been. He was a hard-working union worker with a deep, raspy voice. Although at times he was a little rough around the edges, underneath he had a heart of gold.

You never paid when you were with Mitch; even if he didn't have much money, he would give you his last dollar. He took good care of his daughter financially and tried his best to be a good father. Drinking was a major problem for him, though, and often got him into trouble. Once I went to court to speak on his behalf. He was facing a lot of time. He'd resisted arrest and assaulted a police officer. Drinking was the culprit. Mitch would not have done those things sober. He would black out.

When I was sitting in the court room and heard all the charges out loud, it sounded a lot worse. I'm surprised they didn't lock him up for a long time. Apparently, glass plates had been flying, among other things.

I told the judge what a good-hearted man he was and how, when my father passed, he had assured my mother that, if she needed anything, he would be there for her, and he was.

With his court-appointed lawyer representing him, somehow Mitch caught a break. He did some time, but not as much. Did he learn? Do we ever?

"Hi, Mitch—it's Don. Do you want to go to the *Sopranos* finale with me at Satin Dolls? I can't find anyone to go with, and Sharon said it was okay."

"Are you *kidding* me? Come get me."

When we walked in, the place was packed, better than I thought. Everyone was there—the young, the old. There was a gigantic screen, so the whole place could enjoy the ending. A Tony Soprano look-alike was circling the bar, talking to the crowd. The strippers were dancing seductively, along with great music. The place was full of energy.

Mitch bought us drinks and shots. We were taking it all in and having a blast. Then the lights dimmed, and we all knew the show was about to start. When the opening song came on, the whole place went wild.

Mitch told me he'd run out of money; he had dropped a lot of cash by then. I took out my card and put it on the bar. Mitch looked over at me, and a big grin spread over his face. We were having too much fun, and this party wasn't over.

We were soon enough coming to the end of the show. Everyone in the bar was watching intently to see how it was going to end. The Tony Soprano look-alike kept trying to get me to go home with him, talking while I was trying to watch. I'm surprised he was, because it looked like Mitch and I were together. After a while Mitch said, "Hey, Tony . . .take a walk."

He looked at him and left.

"Mitch," I laughed, "be nice."

"I guess he thought he's the real Tony Soprano," he laughed back, "and you're going to roll on your back and spread your legs for him or something." (Laughing)

The final scene started to roll. Tony walks into the diner. He scopes out the place. He sits down and puts a coin in the juke box, and Journey starts to play. Carmela walks in, and as she passes, I spot the two extras I was talking to at Holsten's sitting in the booth. I was excited for them but, I must admit, a little jealous.

A.J.'s there; so is the guy in the Members Only jacket. Tony's daughter is on her way. I'm so wasted. She's trying to park the car.

The next thing I knew, the place went black.

"What happened? Did the power go out?" I heard somebody say

Mitch exclaimed, "What the fuck?"

I heard a host of mixed reactions from the crowd.
"That's it? That's how it's going to end?"
"*Nooo*. Really?"
"Man, you're kidding me?"
"That was *awesome*," one guy would shout.

But everyone agreed it was a great last episode. How could it not be? It had been one of the best-written shows on television, with the most talented actors. And Mitch and I had the best time. I loved the whole thing, ending and all.

As we were leaving, reporters were waiting outside. One came right up to me and asked me what I thought about the ending. "What was the reaction inside?" he wanted to know.

"It was a mixed reaction," I said, "but I *loved* it! It was *awesome!*"

I think that's what I said. Honestly, I was a little buzzed, but it was something along those lines.

As I stood there, bright lights and camera on me, microphone in front of my mouth as I spoke, it couldn't have been more fitting that I was being interviewed. I felt like I was part of a movie. It was as if someone had written a script, and my whole journey was just falling into place.

The next morning, I went to the mall. A guy who had a stand selling mugs and t-shirts saw me. He knew me from the business I often give him. In a cute little accent, he called out, "I saw you on TV. I saw you on TV! They give you wrong name."

"Where were you when *The Sopranos* aired their last episode?"

"I was at the Bada-Bing. . . . Where else would I be?"

38

NURSE RATCHET

THE DRUG WILL TRY ANYTHING to make its way back into your life. People, places, and things might sound repetitious to a user, but it's so very true to maintain sobriety. Recovery will give you the tools, but it's up to you if you're going to use them. You may not believe that one drink could lead you down the same road. Some must find out for themselves. One can only hope it's not their last chance before they finally get it.

They say God sends you a couple of lifeboats at times, and that it's up to you to get into one of them. I bought a new phone and had to change over all my numbers. Only one was missing when I went to dial it: Lucky's. I quickly—frantically—returned to the phone store. I had them search for it, claiming it was a very important number. The only one missing. . .if *that's* not a sign, I don't know what is.

I don't know how, but the drug found its way briefly back in my life. I finally stopped for good after yet another humiliating experience involving Billy. I used the tools I had learned to clear my life of that seductive yet destructive drug. With all of it behind me, though, I managed to mess up my mental health. I was not feeling well and had to see a doctor. I was referred to a female doctor, clearly overworked and not very nice.

I went to the appointment filled with anxiety. My pocketbook was filled with empty medicine bottles that had all been legally prescribed. I looked disheveled. I was not in good shape. I had only been taking the pills I had been prescribed, but I guess to her I was something else.

"Look at this," she began in a snooty voice. "How many bottles do you have in here? What are you, shopping medication? What is this?" She looked in my bag. "Let's see what you're taking."

I didn't know you were even allowed to get into someone's private prescription history, but somehow she did through the computer. "Ah, Xanax," she murmured, and looked up at me. "How many of those do you take? Huh?"

My anxiety shot through the roof. Who was this person, Nurse Ratchet, the psycho nurse from *One Who Flew Over the Cuckoo's Nest*? I hadn't done any drugs in a very long time. Why was this *happening* to me? Why *now*? *Punishment*, that's what it is, I concluded. I'm being punished for all the hurt I caused for my foolish mistake.

The next couple of days were hell. I couldn't sleep. Nurse R. had given me a new medication that made me feel like I was going to jump out of my skin. I started to have a hard time breathing. *Look what I did to myself.*

The following day, I was walking around the house and

having a terrible time. I couldn't catch my breath. My mother was on the phone with my aunt, when I began to panic. "Mom, Mom!" I exclaimed, tapping her shoulder. "Call the ambulance! I can't *breathe*."

"Gerry, I have to go," she said, and immediately called them; I was gasping for air.

"What did I *do* to myself?"

The police arrived first and gave me some oxygen, I was so scared, I couldn't get enough.

BIG DOG CAME INTO THE EMERGENCY ROOM with my young nephew in tow. With an extreme worried look, he asked, "Are you alright, Aunt Don?"

I hated that he had to see me like that—the aunt that he used to look up to and admire, lying on a gurney, trying to breathe. All I knew was that my condition was a result of very bad decision making, not to mention complete and utter stupidity.

My mother followed shortly after; she was right by my side as always. I was trying to get every bit of oxygen out of the mask that was over my face. I can't *breathe*. . . *someone help me!* I tried to shout out, but nothing came out.

They gave me something to calm me down. I started to breathe better but knew it was just temporary. "Mom, what am I going to do?" I asked when I could finally speak, tears rolling down my eyes. I knew I couldn't go home in that condition. But I was scared and didn't want to go into the hospital either.

"What choice do you have?" she said in her caring way.

"They could help you get on the right medication."

I had been on the right medication and was feeling good coming out of rehab, but I'd gone back to the drug, which led to this mental horror I was stuck with on that gurney.

I had the paper in front of me to sign myself in. I honestly had a hard time moving the pen, and I'm not being dramatic. But I signed; I had no choice.

Anxiety-filled, I arrived, escorted by wheelchair, on the ward. As they wheeled me in, I began to look around. It looked a little better than the last one I attended. Pictures of the staff hung on the wall. I made my way down the line of faces. I froze in a blank stare at one. *Oh, no! Not her—Nurse Ratchet! Are you kidding me?* I thought. *This is like a bad dream.* My anxiety level was off the charts. My session with her had actually contributed to my demise, and there she was.

Luckily, she was not working during my stay, but I *did* go see her after.

"Oh, so you were in the *hospital?*" she asked in that sarcastic voice.

I told her that I hadn't felt good on the medication she'd given me. She only upped the dose. When she saw the medication that the hospital had prescribed for me, to help me sleep, she wanted to do away with it. I pleaded with her to reconsider, considering sleep was my only relief and I didn't want to be up all night.

"This stuff will put one hundred pounds on you. You will get diabetes and lose an arm. You're borderline—do you want to lose and arm?

"I can't be *up* all night! *Please*—I *need* this medication.

Please! I can't sleep without it. It's the only relief I get."

"Do you want to *lose an arm?*"

"The doctors said I could continue taking it when I left the hospital. You could call them if you want."

"Oh, really? *That's* what they said?"

"Why are you being so nasty? What is *wrong* with you?"

She gave me the sleep medication, but I left there on medication that was clearly disagreeing with me. I spent the next year taking it in fear something else might make me feel worse. It was a year of hell. I would go to the gym after taking it and jump on the treadmill, saying my prayers over and over, asking God to help me. The anxiety wore off at night, my only time of peace.

Nurse R. was right about one thing—the sleeping medication *did* put about sixty-five pounds on me.

At the end of my rope, I sought help elsewhere. Anne, a wonderful counselor, saw my tears of pain. She immediately took me by the hand and led me down the hall to the door of a great psychiatrist. He put me on the correct medication. I will be forever grateful to both.

Did I learn my lesson? Yes, I did, but maybe that's what it had to take. The pain of depression and anxiety is so great that you don't want to ever travel down any road that's going to lead you to it. Maybe that extra year was an insurance policy for me in case it ever crept back into my mind. Let me tell you, it sure as hell worked. I have God to thank too for the peace I'm in now.

39

GOODBYE

I WAS SLOWLY PUTTING MY LIFE back together, the new suite of medications I was on was finally starting to take effect. The journey of being an extra in all those movies and television shows was an experience that I will not soon forget. Meeting legends Like Robin Williams and witnessing their magic is like winning a golden backstage pass.

Although I did not get a picture with Tony Soprano, my journey was worth it just to have him walk into the room that day. I so wished I had taken the opportunity to tell him how far I had gone to finally meet him and what a superb actor he was, but I hadn't, for whatever reason. I thought that, maybe, one day our paths would cross again. I imagined that in ten or fifteen years, he might be doing a Broadway play, and that I would conveniently catch him outside and finally take a picture with him. I would tell him my crazy story too, and how, inadvertently, he'd gotten me through one of the worst times of my life.

Years later, I found myself sitting in a coffee shop, reading a book I was trying to finish that day, when a group of women came in and sat down at the table next to mine. They were a little noisy, talking and laughing, a bit too loud for the quiet atmosphere I was hoping to experience. They spoke about what was going on with each of them. I couldn't help but half-listen.

"I went out with Scott last night—my mother-in-law watched the kids. It was so nice to have a couple of hours of total freedom."

"You're so lucky you have your mother-in-law. It's so hard to find a good babysitter."

Then I heard a third voice abruptly blurt out, "Hey, did you hear that James Gandolfini died?"

I can't explain what happened to me at that moment— I felt as if I had been air-kicked in the stomach. I just froze.

"Oh, no! Really?"

"Yeah—a heart attack, in Italy. He was with his son."

A tremendous wave of sadness came over me. I just sat there, trying to process it.

"Oh, no. I *loved* him...that's *terrible*."

Their voices seemed to fade away. I continued to sit there—I don't remember for how long. I didn't know what I was feeling. I didn't understand the connection I seem to now have had to this man, so I didn't understand the loss I felt.

"Uncle Leo, it's Don. I'm so upset...did you hear James Gandolfini died?"

"Yes, I heard."

"I can't believe it. I can't believe he died. A heart

attack. Do you believe it? I'm so upset. I can't believe how upset I am."

"*Do-on*, he was on *television*. Why are you getting this upset over someone on TV? Worry about real people, real people in your life."

"I *am* upset about it! I'm allowed to be upset, Uncle Leo."

"Don't you have enough in life to worry about without finding things to get upset over? He's not *real*—Tony Soprano's not a *real person*. You don't even know him and you're getting yourself so upset over it."

I hung up on him. In all fairness, he had lost five people, including my father, who was his best friend, within four years, so, looking back, I get where he was coming from. Uncle Leo probably hadn't been the best person to call.

It was all over the news. The next day I was on my way to the store and happened to see Satin Dolls, which was on the other side of the highway, and noticed there was something written on the high billboard. I made a U-turn and decided to go there. I got out of the car and looked up at the sign. In bold black letters, the legend read *Thank You, Jimmy. Farewell, Boss.* I stood there staring at the sign. I didn't even know the man, and I felt this way; I couldn't even imagine how those who did must be feeling. I was sad for his family, sad for his friends, and sad that I never got to share a smile with my favorite actor.

40

L'ULTIMO CAPITOLO

I HAVE LEARNED A LOT OF THINGS on my long journey. I was looking for someone to blame for my turbulent childhood. The fact is, there is no *one* person to blame. What happened in my life can be traced back through many generations of dysfunction. I had an opportunity to speak to some of my tormenters as adults and learned something about their own horrendous home lives—neglect, sexual and both physical and mental abuse, and the resulting rage spread to some who could brush it off and others to whom it became a permanent open wound in their adult lives. It's not only the victim who needs help; so does the tormenter.

Billy grew up in a house touched by addiction. He had a wonderful, caring mother but had a lot of heartache in his younger years. He initially beat the odds and exceeded all expectations and became well-off and successful. Later in his life, though, the pain of his past that he had buried for so long caught up with him.

The last time I saw Billy was in court, for child support issues. He was still struggling and looked terrible. I hope one day, with the help of God, he will take the steps to recover. I know he has tried in the past. It would be great, after all these years, to see him finally set free.

"Billy," I said, as I sat beside him, "you have to stop. Something terrible is going to happen to you...*please!*"

"I know. I know...but it's been so many years."

He once jokingly said to me that he was going to write a book called *Rags to Riches to Rags*.

I laid my hand on top of his. As soon as I touched him, I felt that same love and connection I always had.

"Billy, I'm thinking of writing a story. Do you want to know how it ends?"

"How?"

I looked at him with tears in my eyes and said, "That's going to completely up to you."

IN A PERFECT WORLD, YOUNG PEOPLE would not have to be afraid, young hearts to be tarnished, young spirits to be broken. But we don't live in a perfect world, which we have all been told right from the beginning.

Jim Carey said, "The effect you have on others is the most valuable currency there is."

We have all been hurt, hurt other people, and done things we regret. Jim Carey is right: Having everything is not the answer. Although we cannot erase our wounds or mistakes from the past, I believe forgiveness, gratitude, and making one person smile in the course of your day are a good start to healing and the path to true happiness.

As for all the other great actors, directors, and writers past and present of *The Sopranos*, I would need a separate book to write about each and every one of you.

David Chase, you are a talented, brilliant man. You created a masterpiece. The ending was the best. Don't let anyone tell you any differently. Thirteen years later, people are still talking about it.

As for James Gandolfini, I want to thank him for getting me through one of the darkest times of my life. Although it was a bizarre quest, it led me to meet the most interesting people, go to great places, and, in the end, bring my soul back to life.

"You never fail until you stop trying."
—*Albert Einstein*

Acknowledgments

I would like to thank the most important person in this world to me, my daughter. She is the shining light in my life that never goes out—supportive, loving, strong, and creative. She is truly the best thing that ever happened to me.

My family and friends for always being there for me, especially my mother for her unconditional love and forgiveness.

A shout out to these special people: Kathy, Vetka, Shal, Gerry, Lisa, Scott, Abi, Vinnie, and Sandhya, for all their incredible kindness and encouragement. Thank you so much.

Jim Carey, thank you for sharing your experience regarding "the universe." I followed your lead and was amazed how everything just magically fell into place. Your enlightenment on what will and will not bring us happiness has, I'm sure, changed the course of many for the better.

Oprah Winfrey, thank you for dedicating your life and sharing your innermost personal experiences in order to show others that they are not alone and can always rise up and accomplish anything.

To my editor, Barry Sheinkopf, for taking the time and having the patience to help me create a book I could be proud of.

I want to thank David Chase and all the seasons' casts, writers, directors, producers, and crews of *The Sopranos*. It was an incredible ride.

Last but not least, I would like to thank all the background (extras) for their hard work on all movies and television shows. You are an important part of every project. Take a bow.

www.ingramcontent.com/pod-product-compliance
Lightning Source LLC
Chambersburg PA
CBHW030150100526
44592CB00009B/214